Our Early Female Novelists, and Other Essays

Alexander Malcolm Williams

Copyright © BiblioLife, LLC

BiblioLife Reproduction Series: Our goal at BiblioLife is to help readers, educators and researchers by bringing back in print hard-to-find original publications at a reasonable price and, at the same time, preserve the legacy of literary history. The following book represents an authentic reproduction of the text as printed by the original publisher and may contain prior copyright references. While we have attempted to accurately maintain the integrity of the original work(s), from time to time there are problems with the original book scan that may result in minor errors in the reproduction, including imperfections such as missing and blurred pages, poor pictures, markings and other reproduction issues beyond our control. Because this work is culturally important, we have made it available as a part of our commitment to protecting, preserving and promoting the world's literature.

All of our books are in the "public domain" and some are derived from Open Source projects dedicated to digitizing historic literature. We believe that when we undertake the difficult task of re-creating them as attractive, readable and affordable books, we further the mutual goal of sharing these works with a larger audience. A portion of BiblioLife profits go back to Open Source projects in the form of a donation to the groups that do this important work around the world. If you would like to make a donation to these worthy Open Source projects, or would just like to get more information about these important initiatives, please visit www.bibliolife.com/opensource.

Our Early Female Novelists

And other Essays

By
A. M. Williams, M.A.

Principal, Church of Scotland Training College, Glasgow

Glasgow
James MacLehose and Sons
Publishers to the University
1904

NOTE

'*Our Early Female Novelists*' appeared in *Cornhill*, '*Pope*' in *The Gentleman's Magazine*, '*Emily Brontë*' in *Temple Bar*, '*Some Characteristics of Scott's Poetry*' in *The Scots Magazine*, and are now reprinted by kind permission. '*Zola's Theory of the Novel*' is practically a review of that writer's '*Le Roman Expérimental*' and '*Les Romanciers Naturalistes.*'

CONTENTS

	PAGE
OUR EARLY FEMALE NOVELISTS,	1
POPE,	33
EMILY BRONTË,	65
SOME CHARACTERISTICS OF SCOTT'S POETRY,	87
ZOLA'S THEORY OF THE NOVEL,	117

# Our Early Female Novelists

OUR EARLY FEMALE NOVELISTS

In the history of English story-telling an altogether notable place is occupied by Chaucer's *Canterbury Tales*. They are remarkable not only as masterpieces of narrative, but as containing both description of incidents and delineation of manners; not only as triumphs of literary expression, but as giving artistic form both to the romance of chivalry and to the tale of common life. Wholly wonderful it is that at so early a period such directness of movement and perfection of style, such vividness of portraiture and realism of incident, are found in verse, while centuries pass before similar excellences are found in prose.

It is, indeed, peculiarly interesting to contrast Chaucer's practice with the subsequent course of English fiction. He sets his wits against the absurdities of the popular metrical romance, and jingles gaily along in the Rime of Sir Thopas till Harry Bailey, whose 'eres aken with the drasty speche,' pulls him up with an impatient ' na moore of this for Goddes dignitee,' but the merry ridicule glanced harmlessly from the garrulous tellers of long-winded stories, who continued to delight many generations of auditors; the seventeenth century loved such romances as Boyle's *Parthenissa*, and patient readers traced to the abrupt close its devious wandering in the regions of interminable talk and episode.

When Chaucer abandoned his burlesque and took up the heavy tale of Melibeus, he inflicted on his audience a sample of that allegorical didacticism which long clung like a burr to the skirts of prose fiction; throughout mediæval times the allegory followed hard after the story-teller and compelled him to moralise.

In view, however, of the early course of English fiction, the most interesting feature in the *Canterbury Tales* is their intense realism, their free transcription of the actual life of ordinary folk. They abound in that unconventional treatment of man which Thackeray praised in Fielding and desiderated in the modern novel, and illustrate to the full Carlyle's words, 'the poet, we imagine, can never have far to seek for a subject: the elements of his art are in him and around him on every hand.'

But the prose story-tellers were slow to take the lesson to themselves; till the seventeenth century they made only sporadic and short-lived visits to the firm mainland of nature; they preferred to dwell on the floating islands of legend and romance. In the seventeenth century, however, writers seem to have become fully alive to the interest peculiar to real life, and there appear faint foreshadowings of the modern novel.

The Duchess of Newcastle has some claim to honourable mention for her *CCXI. Sociable Letters* (1664). This lady, whom, in her own delightful language, 'it pleased God to command His servant Nature to endue with a poetical and philosophical genius,' was genius enough to see that letters to be readable need not be authentic, and so to secure the credit of being the first to employ a device that since her time has played a large part in prose fiction. She may be allowed, therefore, to introduce the women novelists of the seventeenth and eighteenth centuries; she herself would doubtless lay some stress on her tales in prose as giving her a title to rank among the very earliest novel-writers, but the Illustrissima Heroina (to quote one of the many flattering titles bestowed on her) is not at her best in such performances as *The Converts in Marriage.*

A much more important figure in the beginnings of the English novel is Mrs. Aphra Behn (1640-1689), whose personal history is quite as interesting as any of her stories. Her father, a Mr. Johnson, had influence enough to get himself appointed lieutenant-general of Surinam, and he set sail for the New World, taking his wife and children with him. Mr. Johnson did not live to see the regions he had been sent to rule, but his wife and children spent some years in the beautiful and romantic scenery of Surinam, and there Aphra found the materials of her best novel, *Oroonoko.* The time had not yet come when description of Nature was a recognised feature in a story, but *Oroonoko* contains one or two passages where an attempt is made to reveal to the people of England the beauties of Surinam. These passages have been praised for their 'careless and picturesque power,' but possibly the second epithet is less deserved than the first.

Moreover, one is bound to say that Mrs. Behn's imagination is apt to enter into the record of her experiences. When after her return to England she had the honour of telling her adventures to Charles II., she included among the fauna of South America snakes of terrific dimensions, but a certain licence has always been accorded to the retailers of snake stories. Her most extraordinary traveller's tale is her account of what she saw on her voyage from Antwerp to England. How many among those that go down to the sea in ships have seen floating on the waves 'a four-square floor of various coloured marble, from which ascended rows of fluted and twisted pillars, embossed round with climbing vines and flowers, and waving streamers, that received an easy motion in the air; upon the pillars a hundred little Cupids clambered with fluttering wings'! Little wonder, surely, that following the disappearance of this strange pageant came a violent storm, and Aphra and her companions suffered shipwreck.

There is room for doubting whether Mrs. Behn put into any of her stories as much imagination as adorns the annals of her adventures. For her peculiar claim to attention is that at a time when the heroic romance was in fashion, she went for her characters and incidents to real life. When she appeared in London after her sojourn in Surinam, her good looks, her ready wit, and her lively conversation carried society by storm. She is described as 'a handsome dark girl, with a clear forehead, fine eyes, a full and merry mouth, an animated though voluptuous countenance, and a quick and ready tongue.' The merry monarch himself was charmed with the vivacious Astræa, and asked her to give to the world the moving narrative of the slave prince *Oroonoko*.

This is her best novel, and is in fact a striking book. Its sympathetic story of the high-souled African treacherously lured to the ignominy of slavery, of the sad fate of his faithful Imoinda, and of his own most cruel death, was possibly more rousing than even *Uncle Tom's Cabin*, and its power to touch the heart was greatly increased when Southerne dramatised and presented to the eyes of excited audiences the horrors of slavery. When Mrs. Behn's shortcomings are remembered against her *Oroonoko* should be put to her credit; it is instinct with real feeling and womanly sympathy. 'If,' says Miss Kavanagh, 'if she erred grievously, if she offended delicacy and morality itself by pictures not merely coarse but corrupting, it must never be forgotten that in this sense of the heroic, of all that is noble and manly, she was truly great; whether she invented or merely appreciated *Oroonoko*, her merit is none the less.'

In London the lively Astræa was besieged with suitors, but though her *Letters to a Gentleman* show that when her feelings were really moved she was quite reckless, she was as a rule well able to take care of herself; and she fixed on the oldest, Mr. Behn, a rich London merchant of Dutch origin, who presently died and left her to widowhood and competence.

In 1666 Aphra was sent by the King to Holland to watch the movements of the Dutch, and making Antwerp her head-quarters she set to work with considerable skill. Among her Dutch admirers was a Van der Albert, a man of position and importance, out of whom she wormed that De Witt and

De Ruyter were planning an attack on the English shipping in the Thames. This vital news was at once sent to England only to be ridiculed, and Mrs. Behn, disgusted at the stupidity of the English ministers, turned from politics to domestic intrigue.

Her handling of her Dutch lovers, Van der Albert and Van Bruin, is full of the boisterous, broad fun that riots in her best comedies, though it is conspicuously absent from her novels. They prefer the tragic and the sentimental, though it should be noted that *The Adventures of the Black Lady* has a distinctly comical ending. At Antwerp Mrs. Behn got the groundwork of her second best novel, *The Fair Jilt*, the history of a depraved and heartless coquette. Her disfame as a dramatist has been handed down in Pope's well-known line:

> The stage how loosely does Astræa tread,

and no defence can be offered for the gratuitous indecency of her plays: she certainly did her best to add to the iridescent filth of the Restoration drama. But her novels are not to be put on the same black list: they are indelicate and coarse, it is true, but not to an extent that outraged contemporary taste.

While the plays treat of mere animal passion, the novels teach that women do not deserve to prosper when they are false to true love. In addition to their realism, these novels possess the merit of lively narrative, and make some attempt to portray distinct characters and to analyse emotion.

As has already been suggested, there was realism before the day of *Oroonoko*; very striking examples indeed are found in some of the Elizabethan writers: it did not become a fashion, but showed itself only intermittently and tentatively. On the other hand, its appearance in Mrs. Behn's stories marked the beginning of a reign that lasted far into the eighteenth century; by that time the inevitable reaction had set in, and the swing of the literary pendulum revived romanticism and gave birth to the School of Terror.

A writer that floated high on the rising tide of realism, and in her lifetime achieved both notoriety and reputation, was Mrs. De La Rivière Manley. Her importance in her own world is attested by the frequent occurrence of her name in contemporary literature, and the notice taken of her by men of letters. For her tragedy of *Lucius*, Prior wrote the epilogue; in Pope's charming burlesque, when the Baron carries off 'the sacred hair,' he assigns to himself an immortality equal to that of Mrs. Manley's famous budget of scandal.

> As long as *Atalantis* shall be read,
> . . . . . .
> So long my honour, name, and praise shall live.

In Swift's *Journal to Stella* there are noticeably frequent references to Mrs. Manley—not always complimentary, for he thinks ill both of her spelling and of her personal appearance. Under date January 26, 1711-12, he writes: 'Poor Mrs. Manley, the author, is very ill of a dropsy and sore leg; the printer tells me he is afraid she cannot live long. I am heartily sorry for her; she has very generous principles for one of her sort, and a great deal of good sense and invention. She is about forty, very homely, and very fat.' An earlier passage in the *Journal* testifies to her readiness of pen: 'I forgot to tell you that yesterday was sent me a narrative printed, with all the particulars of Harley's stabbing. I had not time to do it myself, so I sent my hints to the author of *Atalantis*, and she has cooked it into a sixpenny pamphlet in her own style.'

Of this once well-known writer there is little good to say: her life was vicious, and so are her books. Finding people eager to read what was true, or might be true, she fed 'the better vulgar' with a succession of scandalous memoirs and very indecent stories. Her *Atalantis* (1709), a grossly immoral book, which satirised with merciless freedom many of the best-known personages of the day, had a great vogue, its prurient gossip attracting readers with a taste for literary carrion. It brought the author within reach of the law; but the legal proceedings failed of their intent, both retrospective and prospective, and Mrs. Manley continued to make highly-seasoned revelations about herself and about other people. Among her revelations is her opinion of her personal appearance. Speaking of herself under the fictitious name of 'Rivella,' she says: 'Till she grew fat there was not, I believe, any defect to be found in her body; her lips admirably coloured, her teeth small and even; a breath always sweet; her complexion fair and fresh.... Her hands and arms have been publicly celebrated: it is certain that I never saw any so well turned; her neck and breasts have an established reputation for beauty and colour; her feet small and pretty.' One must, in fairness, recall this also as often as one recalls Swift's description of 'Rivella' as 'very homely and very fat.'

Her *Power of Love, in Seven Novels*, may be regarded as an attempt at fictitious narrative divorced from satire : it cannot be regarded as in any way redeeming her reputation, for Mrs. Manley's ideal of love is essentially coarse and sensual. Yet with all her imperfections on her head, Mrs. Manley may not be lightly passed by in a review of what women have done to develop the novel. She emphasised the interest attaching to fictitious narrative based on veritable experience, and she showed how deadly is satire lurking in fiction like a snake in the grass.

Another conspicuous figure among the women writers of these early days is Eliza Haywood, who has been exposed to the ridicule of all time by being offered in the *Dunciad* as the less disgraceful prize in a certain Rabelaisian contest.

> See in the circle next Eliza plac'd,
> Two babes of love close clinging to her waist;
> Fair as before her works she stands confessed,
> In flowers and pearls by bounteous Kirkall dressed.

She has been called 'perhaps the most voluminous female writer this kingdom ever produced,' but it cannot be said that she used her pen to any good purpose. One need not accept in its entirety the accusation that she is one of 'those shameless scribblers who, in libellous memoirs and novels, reveal the faults or misfortunes of both sexes, to the ruin of public fame or disturbance of private happiness,' but it must be confessed that she claims the contemporary privilege of calling a spade a spade. Withal, Mrs. Haywood's *Betsy Thoughtless* (1751) is a book that throws valuable light on the manners of its age. Like Madame D'Arblay's *Evelina*, parts of which it has been supposed to have suggested, *Betsy Thoughtless* is rich in illustration of life in the eighteenth century, and from the standpoint of the early years of the twentieth century one views with amazement the conduct of the men and women of a hundred and fifty years ago. Pope declared that

> Vice is a monster of so frightful mien
> As to be hated needs but to be seen,

and cynics would fain assert that we of this generation have simply disguised the monster, who is as lusty as he was in Mrs. Haywood's time; but even cynics will not assert that women are now subject to the contemptuous treatment of those shameless days. Directly and indirectly the literature of the eighteenth century treats woman as an inferior creature made for man's pleasure. When Milton makes Eve say to Adam—

> O thou for whom
> And from whom I was form'd, flesh of thy flesh,
> And without whom am to no end,

he enunciates a doctrine that long governed and perverted the sexual relation. Addison habitually treats woman as a somewhat troublesome domestic pet, while the realistic novels of the eighteenth century represent her as the temporary object of insulting pursuit.

There is an unconscious admission of this purely physical estimate of women in a sentence in Miss Fielding's *David Simple*: '[David Simple's] mother was a downright country-woman, who originally got her living by plain work; but, being handsome, was liked by Mr. Simple'; and it is noteworthy that the earliest women novelists did very little to maintain the honour of their sex. Not till we come to the novels of Charlotte

Smith (died 1806) do we find a deliberate attempt to represent woman as demanding attention by intellectual and moral qualities.

Betsy Thoughtless was written towards the close of Mrs. Haywood's life, and before it appeared the reading public was in possession of Richardson's *Pamela* and *Clarissa Harlowe*, of Fielding's *Joseph Andrews* and *Tom Jones*, and of Smollett's *Roderick Random*; that is to say, it was not published till the modern novel was fully developed.

Her early novels have little merit, and are inferior in importance to Miss Fielding's *David Simple*, which was issued in 1744, and, on historical grounds, must be regarded as an important book in the history of the novel. Richardson said of it: 'What a knowledge of the human heart! Well might a critical judge of writing say, as he did to me, that your late brother's knowledge of it was not (fine writer as he was) comparable to yours. His was but as the knowledge of the outside of a clockwork machine, while yours was that of all the finer springs and movements of the inside.' This is a judgment considerably overstrained; but, as a matter of fact, *David Simple* shows notable power of mental analysis, and an effective command of satire. Read, for example, this of a girl that has sacrificed liking to vanity: 'For now, that she thought him irretrievable, she fancied in him she had lost everything valuable; and though that very day all her grief had been how to get rid of him, yet, now he was gone, she would have sacrificed (for the present) even her darling vanity if she could have brought him back again'; and this of a man, old and ugly, who wished to marry: 'He was not afraid of being refused, for he had money enough to have bought a woman of much higher rank.' And there is a strong note in the words, 'David Simple was convinced that no circumstances of time, place, or station made a man either good or bad, but the disposition of his own mind.' Unfortunately, the book is a total failure in point of construction. The author had the ability to produce a book strong in characterisation, but the influence of the picaresque school of romance, the school of Gil Blas, led her to introduce a series of incidents which fail to interest the reader.

Satire found another employment in the hands of Mrs. Charlotte Lennox, who in *The Female Quixote* (1752) turned it with strong effect against the extravagance of the Scuderi romance. A special interest attaches to this book from the fact that the great Cham of literature himself is supposed to have written the last chapter, where the heroine is reclaimed from the dominion of absurdity. Mrs. Lennox was indeed a high favourite with Dr. Johnson, who has recorded that 'he dined at Mrs. Garrick's with Mrs. Carter, Miss Hannah More, and Miss Fanny Burney; three such women are not to be found. I know not where I could find a fourth, except Mrs. Lennox, who is superior to them all.'

This is praise from Sir Hubert Stanley, but the recipient seems to have deserved the esteem in which she was held by her contemporaries. She was an industrious and in some directions a meritorious writer, whose work enlisted the sympathy of others besides Johnson. Goldsmith wrote an epilogue for her comedy *The Sister*, and the Earl of Orrery contributed to her version of Brunnoy's *Greek Theatre*. An interesting incident in her life is the banquet given by the Ivy Club in honour of the publication of her *Memoirs of Harriet Stuart*. She and her husband were present at the feast, which lasted all night, and included among its attractions a large apple-pie presented by Dr. Johnson.

Posterity, however, has practically ceased to remember Mrs. Lennox, while it remembers with some distinctness one of the ladies whom Dr. Johnson ranks as her inferiors. Miss Burney, or Madame D'Arblay, retains a place in literature partly by her novels, partly by her exceedingly interesting diary. Nor must it be forgotten that, although *Evelina* appeared so long ago as 1778, there are many people still living who were young men and women when she died. She has been praised by Macaulay for describing real life 'with broad comic humour,' yet in language that is never 'inconsistent with rigid morality or even with virgin delicacy,' and it is true that *Evelina* possesses unique interest as a description of contemporary manners and is free from unnecessary coarseness; it is also true that the author has a keen eye for the ridiculous and a considerable gift of satire.

Nevertheless Madame D'Arblay is not entitled to any high place as a novelist; her constructive skill is small, and her characters are for the most part what Jonson would have called 'humourists,' that is, they are the incarnation of qualities rather than flesh and blood individuals. Moreover, the author herself is a 'humourist,' her ruling passion is a morbid craving to be 'genteel'; she has no mercy for vulgarity or the vulgar, but she fails to see that her own worship of society conventions is itself vulgar. And hence one may doubt the propriety of assigning to her 'broad comic humour'; she was too much of a prig to be possessed of humour, which implicates geniality. Still Madame D'Arblay claims respect on the specific ground that she did much to purify an important form of literature, while she has a certain additional claim to remembrance from her connection with Dr. Johnson. Did not Dr. Johnson kiss her, and has she not recorded, 'To be sure I was a little surprised, having no idea of such facetiousness from him'?

A more likeable personality than the demure Miss Burney is Mrs. Charlotte Smith, a woman on whom had descended many graces of body and of mind, but whom Fate refused any measure of happiness. Married at the age of fourteen to a man of mean and contemptible character, she found herself condemned to an existence of gloom and drudgery. After her father-in-law died, her husband quickly squandered a large inheritance, and found himself in a debtors' prison, where his wife attended him.

From this time onwards Mrs. Smith's lot was to struggle to support herself and her family by hard and unremitting literary labour. Very little has lived of her many and varied productions, and yet she does not deserve to have been so completely forgotten. Mention has already been made of her honourable attempt to raise the estimation of her sex by declining to make the interest of her heroines depend on purely physical attractions, and some credit is also due to her for having been one of the very first writers to employ description to heighten the power of the novel. She seems to have been peculiarly susceptible to the influences of nature, and her writings contain many descriptive passages. The best of her novels is *The Old Manor House* (1793), which may still be read with pleasure; in it her somewhat moderate powers of construction and of character-drawing appear to most advantage, and have produced a really interesting story. She also wrote verses, whose prevailing tone is a gentle melancholy; in lines like these one hears a sigh for the careless joy of her childish years:

> Ah, poor humanity! so frail, so fair,
>   Are the fond visions of thy early day,
> Till tyrant passion and corrosive care
>   Bid all thy fairy colours fade away.
> Another May new buds and flowers will bring,
> Ah! why has happiness no second spring?

Like the present generation, eighteenth century readers were allured to the consideration of grave questions by means of the problem novel, for the era of the French Revolution was a time when the air was full of problems and when quite a vigorous crop of purpose novels sprang up. Among the writers affected by the demand for a return to pure, unsophisticated nature was the beautiful and daring Mrs. Inchbald.

At an early age she was seized with a strong passion for the stage, and twice, while still in her teens, she ran away from home and went to London to see whether Fortune would do for her what application to stage-managers had failed to do. A sufficiently dangerous step this on the part of a young woman who is described as 'tall and slender, with hair of a golden auburn, and lovely hazel eyes, perfect features, and an enchanting countenance.' In her nineteenth year she married, her husband being an actor, and she herself now appeared on the boards. She does not seem to have been a very successful actress, but she was able to make considerable sums by her pen: she was exceedingly well paid for her plays, and very well paid for her two novels, *A Simple Story*, and *Nature and Art*.

In spite of grave defects, for which the imperfect education of the author is so far responsible, these two stories are eminently readable. As has been said by critics, *A Simple Story* is really two stories, and the double plot is handled with some awkwardness; moreover, there is a tendency to exaggeration in the portraiture, a notable example being the character of Sandford, the priest, whose churlishness is overdrawn to the point of childishness, while much of the writing is very raw. Still, the story holds the reader's attention; the chief figure, Miss Milner, is skilfully handled, and the incidents are well chosen and effectively used. The lesson of the story, for it has a moral writ large on it, is that parents are bound to give the most serious consideration to the training of their children.

In *Nature and Art* the moral is of another kind. In it we are invited to despise William, the polished, insincere product of civilisation, and to admire his cousin Henry, the natural man, who cannot understand the hollow refinements of an artificial society. The reader has no difficulty in despising William, but it is not so easy to admire Henry, for in her anxiety to do justice to his transparent honesty, Mrs. Inchbald makes the worthy youth ridiculous. But withal *Nature and Art* is an impressive story, and the author's dramatic experience stands her in good stead in the powerful scene where William, now risen to the bench, passes sentence of death on the wretched woman in the dock, whom he fails to recognise as the hapless victim of his own selfish passion. The conclusion of the book is notable: ' "While I have health and strength," cried the old man, and his son's looks acquiesced in all the father said, "I will not take from any one in affluence what only belongs to the widow, the fatherless, and the infirm ; for to such alone by Christian laws—however custom may subvert them—the overplus of the rich is due." '

Mrs. Inchbald was left a widow when she was only in her twenty-sixth year, and though she was besieged with addresses, honourable and dishonourable, she repulsed them all, and bore herself with prudent wisdom among the distinguished people that gathered round the popular writer. At the same time she seems to have indulged a natural vanity over her good looks, her many conquests, and her noble acquaintances. Her letters tell us that she never gave up the domestic industry that early circumstances had made first necessary and then habitual. 'Last Thursday morning,' she writes, 'I finished scouring my bedchamber, while a coach with a coronet and two footmen waited at the door to take me an airing.'

The time was now come when romanticism, which had had to give way before the tide of realism, was again to assert itself with power. In 1764 Horace Walpole had published his Gothic romance, *The Castle of Otranto*, a book that introduced novel readers to a world very different from that in which they had been wandering under the guidance of the great novelists of the eighteenth century, and by-and-by this new kind of fiction was taken up with much success by two women, Clara Reeve and Mrs. Radcliffe.

The modern reader is prone to grin broadly at Walpole's elaborate machinery for making the flesh creep, and one may doubt whether there were ever readers that were disturbed by a passage like this: ' " Thou art no lawful prince," said Jerome; "thou art no prince—go, discuss thy claim with Frederic; and when that is done——" " It is done," replied Manfred; " Frederic accepts Matilda's hand, and is content to waive his claim, unless I have no male issue." As he spoke these words, three drops of blood fell from the nose of Alfonso's statue.'

The most credulous devourer of romances must have drawn the line at a statue whose nose bled: it is a circumstance almost as ridiculous as the catastrophe in Lewis's *Monk*. In that hysterical romance the demon's flight with the priest is intended to be appalling, but is in fact one of the most laughable things in our literature. However, with all its absurdities, the School of Terror was established, and held its ground till the day of Scott, whose early verse is strongly marked by some of its characteristics.

But Walpole's successors and imitators felt he had made too severe a demand on the imagination of readers, and in her preface to *The Old English Baron*, Clara Reeve points out some defects in *The Castle of Otranto*. 'The machinery is so violent that it destroys the effect it is intended to excite. Had the story been kept within the utmost *verge* of probability, the effect had been preserved, without losing the least circumstance that excites or detains attention.' Miss Reeve's idea was to cut down the supernatural to an irreducible minimum, which 'the gentle reader' might fairly be asked to put up with. But *The Old English Baron* (1777) is not a success in spite of the fact that we are not called upon to stand anything extramundane beyond what might be inventoried as certain hollow groans, one suit of armour, clanking, and one phantom knight.

The book is much less impressive than the more famous *Mysteries of Udolpho* (1794), by Mrs. Radcliffe, who must be allowed to have achieved excellence in the field of art she chose to cultivate, and this both Miss Reeve and Mrs. Radcliffe's imitators failed to do. Every mind is affected—the average mind is very strongly affected—by gloom and expectancy, and of this feeling Mrs. Radcliffe takes skilful advantage. Even ordinary characters, natural incidents and natural scenery, loom large and portentous in the romantic obscurity through which we follow the mysterious windings of the narrative; again and again we seem to strain eye and ear to follow the progress of events, and await the approach of some dread catastrophe.

And, it is important to observe, Mrs. Radcliffe effects all this after parting completely with the supernatural; she is so careful, indeed, to show that terrified suspense may be induced by perfectly natural circumstances that she mars her art and goes far to offend the reader by irritatingly simple explanations of fear-inspiring phenomena. Nevertheless, Mrs. Radcliffe occupies one of the highest positions in the School of Terror, and she has earned her place by genuine merits of composition.

An altogether different interest attaches to the novels of the Sisters Lee, joint authors of a collection of stories called the *Canterbury Tales*. Of these stories all save two were written by Harriet Lee, and to her, as the author of *Kruitzner*, belongs the credit of having inspired Byron's *Werner*. The two sisters deserve to be remembered for the brave way in which they faced the world. Their father had taken to the stage, where he commanded little success, and from him they inherited neither repute nor money: it was to the stage, however, that his daughters were indebted for a secure and honourable provision; the success of Sophia's comedy, *The Chapter of Accidents*, enabled the sisters to set up a school at Bath, and in it they won a competence and general respect. The younger sister, Harriet, was the more voluminous writer: her dramatic work is of no value, but several of her tales are marked by strong interest, and must be regarded as an important contribution to the stream of fiction. Her sister demands special mention as the author of *The Recess* (1785), one of the very earliest and, it must be added, very worst of our historical novels.

With the Sisters Lee we enter the nineteenth century, and they may be allowed to end the list of early female novelists. The last of the *Canterbury Tales* appeared in 1805; nine years later a delighted public was reading *Waverley*. We have therefore reached the period when the English novel entered on its most flourishing days, and now leave it, content to have indicated in some measure what women did to illustrate and develop the capabilities of fiction.

Pope

POPE

THE supreme literary achievement of Pope's age was the polishing of the heroic couplet. In Pope's own hands this form of verse became an instrument of marvellous precision and beauty, lending itself with unique effect to rhetorical point and finish. Our earlier literature no doubt contains many poems in this measure, but in Pope's time new and characteristic features were added, and these it is necessary to examine and appraise. For this purpose we must first acquaint ourselves with the earlier forms of the heroic couplet. This is the metre of most of the *Canterbury Tales*, where it is distinguished by regularity, smoothness, variety of pause, and delicacy of rhyme.

> This passeth yeer by yeer and day by day,
> Til it fil onës, in a morwe of May,

> That Emelye, that fairer was to sene
> Than is the lilyë upon his stalkë grene,
> And fressher than the May with flourës newe,—
> For with the rosë colour stroof hire hewe,
> I noot which was the fýner of hem two,—
> Er it were day, as was hir wone to do,
> She was arisen, and al redy dight;
> For May wole have no slogardrie a nyght.

Curiously enough this finely-developed versification was little used and with small effect by Chaucer's contemporaries and successors. We do not recognise the Chaucerian movement in lines like these from Gawin Douglas:

> And blissful blossoms in the bloomed yard
> Submits their heads in the young sun's safeguard:
> Ive leavès rank o'erspread the barmkin wall;
> The bloomed hawthorn clad his pikes all.

Nor is the Chaucerian movement to be recognised in the couplet as handled by the Elizabethans. Easy flow is the main feature of Jonson's sweet lines:

> I do remember, Marian, I have oft
> With pleasure kist my lambs and puppies˙soft;
> And once a dainty, fine roe-fawn I had,
> Of whose outskipping bounds I was as glad
> As of my health; and him I oft would kiss;
> Yet had his no such sting or pain as this;
> They never prick'd or hurt my heart; and for
> They were so blunt and dull, I wish no more.

> But this that hurts and pricks doth please, this sweet
> Mingled with sour, I wish again to meet:
> And that delay, methinks, most tedious is
> That keeps or hinders me of Karol's kiss.

The same free, 'run-on' verse is found in Marlowe, Chapman, Hall, Donne, and others. This licence, this drawing out of the sense from line to line, is, in the hands of a poet, a fertile liberty, but, in the hands of a poetaster, it tends to yield somewhat invertebrate verse. There is a strong contrast between the nervelessness of Crashaw's lines—

> It is love's great artillery
> Which here contracts itself, and comes to lie
> Close couch'd in your white bosom, and from thence,
> As from a snowy fortress of defence,
> Against the ghostly foe to take your part,
> And fortify the hold of your chaste heart,

and the sharp ring of Waller's *Verses on a War with Spain*:

> Others may use the ocean as their road,
> Only the English make it their abode,
> Whose ready sails with every wind can fly,
> And make a covenant with the inconstant sky;
> Our oaks secure as if they there took root,
> We tread on billows with a steady foot.

Comparing Waller's lines with Crashaw's, we note that, in the second passage, each couplet gives a complete meaning; that the lines, if somewhat mechanical, are neat and clean cut, and that there is a desire to secure point by the play of antithesis. We remark the same qualities in the more highly finished verse of Pope:

> Search, then, the ruling passion: there, alone,
> The wild are constant, and the cunning known;
> The fool consistent, and the false sincere;
> Priests, princes, women, no dissemblers here.

The fashion set by Waller became predominant and exclusive, and the eighteenth century turned out thousands on thousands of skilfully constructed heroic couplets. The superficial merits of this form of verse attract the ear, even when the contents are nonsense. Take for example Thackeray's *Timbuctoo*:

> The day shall come when Albion's self shall feel
> Stern Afric's wrath, and writhe 'neath Afric's steel.
> I see her tribes the hill of glory mount,
> And sell their sugars on their own account;
> While round her throne the prostrate nations come,
> Sue for her rice, and barter for her rum.

This is, of course, mere fooling, but Erasmus Darwin wrote his *Botanic Garden* in sober earnest :

> Hail, adamantine steel! magnetic lord!
> King of the prow, the ploughshare, and the sword!
> True to the pole, by thee the pilot guides
> His steady helm amid the struggling tides;
> Braves with broad sail th' immeasurable sea,
> Cleaves the dark air, and asks no star but thee.

The next four lines treat of the ploughshare, the succeeding four of the sword. When the heroic couplet had become an electuary for conveying instruction, it had evidently exhausted its poetic usefulness, and might fitly make way for new verse-forms. These, however, do not belong here. I return to the heroic couplet as used by Pope.

Professor Minto has remarked that 'five-accent couplets are more suited for comedy and the comic epic than for tragedy and the grand epic.' This distinction, which is sound and valuable, is an excellent guide to the appraising of Pope. In the ever delightful *Rape of the Lock*, the polished verse is in perfect harmony with the subject matter; in the satiric poems the finished balance and point of the expression sends every thrust home.

> Much they extoll'd his pictures, much his seat,
> And flatter'd every day, and some days eat:
> Till, grown more frugal in his riper days,
> He paid some bards with port, and some with praise;
> For some a dry rehearsal was assign'd,
> And others (harder still) he paid in kind.
> Dryden alone (what wonder?) came not nigh,
> Dryden alone escap'd this judging eye;
> But still the great have kindness in reserve.
> He help'd to bury whom he help'd to starve.

In the didactic poems the verse is equally effective: the epigrammatic compactness of the lines is in complete keeping with the character of these works, which are rather collections of maxims than sequacious expositions. And, to go a step further, we feel that the couplet is on a level with the glittering rhetoric of the *Messiah*, and the lofty eloquence that closes the *Dunciad*:

> Lo! thy dread empire, Chaos, is restored;
> Light dies before thy uncreating word;
> Thy hand, great Anarch, lets the curtain fall
> And universal darkness buries all.

But let us test its power to express the deepest emotions, to inspire what Aristotle calls pity and terror. Hear how Pope threatens the 'mean deserter of a brother's blood':

> Thus, if eternal justice rules the ball,
> Thus shall your wives, and thus your children fall;
> On all the line a sudden vengeance waits,
> And frequent herses shall besiege your gates.

This is hardly more impressive than

> Cursed be the man, the poorest wretch in life,
> The crouching vassal to the tyrant wife,

and seems to show that the neat, carefully balanced couplet is inadequate to express strong feeling. We listen in vain for the momentous swell of Milton's sonnet—

> Avenge, O, Lord, thy slaughter'd saints, whose bones
> Lie scattered on the Alpine mountains cold;

or for the threatening roll of Southey's ode—

> Who counsels peace at this momentous hour,
> When God hath given deliverance to the oppress'd
> And to the injured power?

This insufficiency of the heroic couplet is equally manifest when the feeling to be expressed is tender and pathetic:

> So peaceful rests, without a stone or name,
> What once had beauty, titles, wealth, and fame.
> How lov'd, how honour'd once, avails thee not,
> To whom related, or by whom begot;

> A heap of dust alone remains of thee,
> 'Tis all thou art, and all the proud shall be.

The coldness of these lines is not due to the mere fact that pains had been taken with the expression. If we read Landor's equally artistic lines on the death of Rose Aylmer, where almost the same sentiments appear, we hear a more thrilling note:

> Ah, what avails the sceptred race!
> Ah, what the form divine!
> What every virtue, every grace!
> Rose Aylmer, all were thine.

It would appear, then, that the heroic couplet in the brilliant rhetorical form it received at the hands of Pope enhances the effect of most of Pope's writing, but serves to conceal the intrinsic poetry of compositions like the *Elegy* and the *Eloisa to Abelard*.

If we proceed now to enquire what kind of poems Pope wrote, we find ourselves face to face with a very thorny question—the question, namely, of the precise nature of poetry. For Pope can hardly be placed in any of the three recognised poetic classes—the lyric, the epic, the dramatic. Not that he stands wholly outside them all, as he stood in his dream of the Temple of Fame, 'betwixt earth, seas, and skies,' for I do not hold with those who say Pope is not a poet at all. The difficulty arises because Pope's claim to the name poet rests almost entirely on his style, and because his subjects, while they have points of contact with each of the poetic classes, do not pronouncedly and decisively belong to any one of them. At this stage it is in place to ask what are the subjects proper to poetry.

'The Poet,' said Wordsworth, in the famous preface, 'ought especially to take care that, whatever passions he communicates to his reader, those passions, if his reader's mind be sound and vigorous, should always be accompanied with an overbalance of pleasure.' But the pleasure is distinct from that which accompanies the gratification of an appetite, or the securing of some personal advantage. It is pure and refined, free from animalism and selfishness. This unalloyed pleasure is yielded by poetry that conveys the distinctive delights of the eye and the ear.

Now fades the glimmering landscape on the sight,

is exquisitely poetical, and the same praise belongs to Pope's line—

> And the hush'd waves glide softly to the shore.

The pleasures proper to the other senses have animal adjuncts that make them less suitable to poetry, though Keats proves abundantly how far they may be idealised by poetic refinement.

> And still she slept an azure-lidded sleep,
>   In blanched linen, smooth and lavendered,
> While he from forth the closet brought a heap
>   Of candied apple, quince, and plum, and gourd;
> With jellies soother than the creamy curd,
>   And lucent syrops, tinct with cinnamon;
> Manna and dates, in argosy transferred
>   From Fez; and spiced dainties, every one,
> From silken Samarcand to cedared Lebanon.

Compare with this a stroke of realistic coarseness—

> The brawny spearman let his cheek
> Bulge with the unswallow'd piece,

where Tennyson deliberately throws in a hard, unpoetic touch. Poetry, however, is not restricted to the sensuous: supremely beautiful as the *Faery Queene* is, it does not represent the highest achievement of poetic art. The ear is ravished by lines like these:

> And more, to lulle him in his slumber soft,
>   A trickling stream from high rock tumbling down,
> And ever drizzling raine upon the loft,
>   Mixt with a murmuring winde, much like the sowne
> Of swarming bees, did cast him in a swowne.
>   No other noyse, nor people's troublous cryes,
> As still are wont t' annoy the walled towne,
>   Might there be heard: but careless Quiet lyes
> Wrapt in eternall silence, farre from enemies;

but they do not fill the soul like lines of greater argument—like the majestic opening of *Paradise Lost*:

> Of man's first disobedience, and the fruit
> Of that forbidden tree whose mortal taste
> Brought death into the world and all our woe,
> With loss of Eden, till one greater man
> Restore us and regain the blissful seat,
> Sing, Heavenly Muse.

The greatest poetry deals with the greatest themes: it appeals to our deepest emotion, it responds to our intellectual cravings, and inflames us as with the fire of oratory. Yet withal it remains poetry—it does not usurp the functions of the teacher or the orator, its specific and characteristic end is to make whatsoever subject it adorns a source of pure and noble pleasure, by redeeming it from pain and the soilure of grossness and self-regard. This admits of ample and minute discussion and of full exemplification; but one illustration must suffice.

> Then mark'd astronomers with keener eyes
> The moon's refulgent journey through the skies;
> Watch'd the swift comets urge their blazing cars,
> And weigh'd the sun with his revolving stars.

This is certainly not poetry, nor is it very satisfactory as information. If we turn from Darwin to Tennyson, we see with what poetic fitness the latter can use scientific materials:

> While some, whose souls the old serpent long had drawn
> Down, as the worm draws in the wither'd leaf
> And makes it earth, hiss'd each at other's ear
> What shall not be recorded.

Or, to make the contrast sharper by keeping to astronomy, listen to Addison's fine stanza:

> Soon as the evening shades prevail,
> The moon takes up the wondrous tale;
> And nightly to the listening earth
> Repeats the story of her birth.

I now turn to Pope's writings, and take up first the descriptive poems. The *Pastorals* may be dismissed with the remark that their poverty of material should not prevent one from enjoying the polished and pleasing verse:

> Thyrsis, the music of that murm'ring spring
> Is not so mournful as the strains you sing.
> Nor rivers winding thro' the vales below,
> So sweetly warble, or so smoothly flow.

'The design of *Windsor Forest*,' says Dr. Johnson, 'is evidently derived from *Cooper's Hill*, with some attention to Waller's poem on *The Park*; but Pope cannot be denied to excel his masters in variety and elegance, and the art of interchanging description, narrative, and morality.' All this may be conceded without admitting that the poem succeeds in conveying to us the natural charms of the Forest. It 'has the merits both of dignity and of variety,' but it sadly lacks the true note of nature-poetry. What hearty lover of woodland scenery could have written this:

> Here waving groves a chequer'd scene display,
> And part admit, and part exclude the day:
> *As some coy nymph her lover's warm address,*
> *Nor quite indulges, nor can quite repress?*

The second couplet is atrocious. Take again the passage:

> Here in full light the russet plains extend;
> There wrapt in clouds the blueish hills ascend.
> Ev'n the wild heath displays her purple dyes,
> And 'midst the desert fruitful fields arise,
> That crown'd with tufted trees and springing corn,
> Like verdant isles, the sable waste adorn.

The colouring here is ambitious and striking, yet it lacks something: it does not, like Wordsworth's, bring us into the very presence of nature—

> The sun, above the mountain's head,
>   A freshening lustre mellow
> Through all the long green fields has spread,
>   His first sweet evening yellow.

The eye looks through the page where such words are written, and rests with calm delight on the landscape itself. We may test Pope in another way. A brilliant passage in *Windsor Forest* describes the death of a pheasant:

> See! from the brake the whirring pheasant springs,
> And mounts exulting on triumphant wings:
> Short is his joy; he feels the fiery wound,
> Flutters in blood, and panting beats the ground.
> Ah! what avail his glossy, varying dyes,
> His purple crest, and scarlet circled eyes,

The vivid green his shining plumes unfold,
His painted wings, and breast that flames like gold?

Poetry, according to Wordsworth, 'takes its origin from emotion recollected in tranquillity,' and it would not be right to say Pope never felt for the dying bird, but it would be right to say that the reader does not feel for it, that the feeling excited by the passage is admiration for the poet's technique. Compare Burns's treatment of a similar situation:

Go, live, poor wanderer of the wood and field,
  The bitter little that of life remains;
  No more the thickening brakes and verdant plains
To thee shall home, or food, or pastime yield.
Seek, mangled wretch, some place of wonted rest,
  No more of rest, but now thy dying bed!
  The sheltering rushes whistling o'er thy head,
The cold earth with thy bloody bosom prest.

There is a pretty moonlight passage in Pope's translation of the Thebais of Statius:

'Twas now the time when Phœbus yields to night,
And rising Cynthia sheds her silver light,
Wide o'er the world in solemn pomp she drew,
Her airy chariot hung with pearly dew;
All birds and beasts lie hush'd; sleep steals away
The wild desires of men and toils of day,
And brings, descending through the silent air,
A sweet forgetfulness of human care.

But compare this with one Shakespearean line—

> How sweet the moonlight sleeps upon this bank,

and we see that it is without the inner feeling that marks real nature poetry.

What may be called the sentimental poems also suffer from excess of finish; the style obscures the sentiment. This has already been illustrated in the case of the *Elegy*, and *Eloisa to Abelard* is open to the same objection. The grief that longs for death is hardly apparent in Eloisa's language as it appears in Pope:

> I come, I come! prepare your roseate bow'rs,
> Celestial palms, and ever-blooming flow'rs.
> Thither, where sinners may have rest, I go,
> Where flames refin'd in breasts seraphic glow.

As an expression of strong feeling, this is tame and feeble, and comes far short of affecting us like the exceeding bitter cry of Constance:

> Misery's love,
> O, come to me!

But, after all, descriptive and sentimental writing does not form a large part of Pope's poetry. The great bulk of his work is didactic and satiric, and here the heroic couplet is in the most perfect keeping. He also wrote some other kinds of verse, but these, with one illustrious exception, I shall refer to only for incidental illustration. *The Rape of the Lock*, however, deserves separate mention: in its class it is unsurpassable. The trifling affair on which, at Caryll's suggestion, Pope wrote his burlesque, becomes the basis of a poem whose conception, machinery, incidents, and verse are all alike admirable. At the very outset Pope catches the light, airy tone, and makes his points with the neat, delicate touch proper to the mock heroic at its best, and throughout the poem he shows the same easy mastery of his subject and himself.

If any critic chooses to argue, as Taine does, that Pope is in deadly earnest, and is really in a satirical humour, he can, no doubt, point to passages that plausibly support his contention, and harmonise in some degree at least with the general tone of Pope's more bitter verses; but this is to forget that the leopard cannot change his spots, that Pope, even in a playful mood, does not cease to be a 'portentous cub,' and that in sportive moments he is like puss herself, and cannot consent wholly to hide his claws. In fact,

The Rape of the Lock shows us a dangerous satirist condescending to the gayest *persiflage*, but necessarily reminding us now and again of the rock whence he was hewn. The banter is skilfully varied. The mock heroic tone is exactly caught in the description of the Baron's sacrifice:

> For this, ere Phœbus rose, he had implor'd
> Propitious heav'n, and every power ador'd,
> But chiefly Love—to Love an altar built
> Of twelve vast French romances, neatly gilt.
> There lay three garters, half a pair of gloves,
> And all the trophies of his former loves;
> With tender billets-doux he lights the pyre,
> And breathes three am'rous sighs to raise the fire.
> Then prostrate falls, and begs with ardent eyes
> Soon to obtain, and long possess the prize;
> The pow'rs gave ear, and granted half his pray'r,
> The rest, the winds dispersed in empty air.

There is a touch of broad farce in these lines:

> Just where the breath of life his nostrils drew,
> A charge of snuff the wily virgin threw;
> The Gnomes direct, to ev'ry atom just,
> The pungent grains of titillating dust.
> Sudden, with starting tears each eye o'erflows,
> And the high dome re-echoes to his nose.

A couplet like—

> Not louder shrieks to pitying heav'n are cast,
> When husbands, or when lap-dogs breathe their last

reminds us of who is unbending for our entertainment; and I admit there is enough of this tone to have justified the lady in objecting to be quizzed with quite such a lordly air, but Pope did not mean to be ill-natured when he wrote this charming trifle.

The didactic poems would lead to a long and perplexed discussion if they were gravely analysed and criticised as a system of instruction; but to this course there are two sufficient objections: first, critics have shown that Pope really has not a reasoned system of philosophy, that he merely poetises philosophic fragments; secondly, it is not the business of literary criticism to discuss questions of philosophy, though it may consider how far in any given case they lend themselves to literary effect. No doubt the *Essay on Criticism* is, both in form and in substance, within the province of the littérateur, but the exposition of the canons of criticism, like the exposition of the abstract doctrines of ontology and ethics, hardly lends itself to high poetry, though it is capable of artistic expression. So that, ultimately, the whole body of Pope's didactic verse belongs to poetics in virtue of form alone. His opinions on metaphysics, conduct, and æsthetics are in another category. With regard to the form of his didactic poetry, there is not room for two opinions as to its excellence. The lines have been polished and refined till they are positively brilliant; their lustre may be somewhat metallic, but it is unmistakably real and effective. The expression has been pruned till it is the ideal of succinct epigrammatic utterance; indeed, one could adduce cases where compression has been so eagerly sought that grammar and even sense have been sacrificed. The lines are crowded with the artifices of rhetoric—with balance, the condensed sentence, contrast, and epigram; while, considered merely as lines, they are open only to one objection, a certain monotony in the fall of the pause:

> Our depths who fathoms, or our shallows finds,
> Quick whirls, and shifting eddies, of our minds?
> On human actions reason tho' you can,
> It may be Reason, but it is not Man:
> His Principle of action once explore,
> That instant 'tis his Principle no more:
> Like following life thro' creatures you dissect,
> You lose it in the moment you detect.

'If,' says Mr. Leslie Stephen, 'the test of poetry were the power of expressing a theory more closely and pointedly than prose, such writing would take a very high place.' This remark is an apt illustration of relativity, for we at once ask, expressing a theory to whom? Emerson observes that 'the correspondence of Pope and Swift describes mankind around them as monsters,' and we may take it that Pope did not trouble himself to bring his meaning within the comprehension of the man in the street, that he wrote for that society in which he himself, Bolingbroke, and Swift were prominent—for those, in fact, that already knew all he had to say to them, but were willing to be interested in a brilliant re-statement of their philosophic commonplaces. But this view of the case forthwith robs the poems of all practical value as didactics, for they cannot be said to instruct if they appeal only to those that need no instruction. They could be proved to be almost useless as a means of instructing those that do need instruction. It might be said of the authors of the Pope school that 'instead of writing to express things, they write to say them well.' And they hit the mark. Pope cannot be accused of being

> Pleas'd with a work where nothing's just or fit,
> One glaring chaos and wild heap of wit.

The *Essay on Criticism*, for example, is, to those familiar with the matters treated, a delightful review of the subject.

> Some beauties yet no precepts can declare,
> Yet there's a happiness as well as care.
> Music resembles Poetry; in each
> Are nameless graces which no methods teach,
> And which a master-hand alone can reach.
> If, where the rules not far enough extend
> (Since rules were made but to promote their end),
> Some lucky Licence answer to the full
> Th' intent propos'd, that Licence is a rule.

This is accepted doctrine, but we admire Pope's way of putting it. The *Essay on Criticism* deals with a subject familiar to Pope, and hence leaves a deeper impression of sincerity than the philosophical poems, where we suspect at times that Pope is somewhat out of his depth. And even when we do not suspect that, we are apt to think the author's heart is more in the expression than in the sentiment. Take an example:

> Honour and state from no condition rise;
> Act well your part, there all the honour lies.

Is Pope in downright earnest here? as much in earnest as Burns in the independent cry:

> The pith o' sense, and pride o' worth,
> Are higher rank than a' that?

Or is he giving a neat turn to a pious opinion, intended for discussion among philosophers, not for practical application? Again and again, when we come across sentiments like that written in the Twickenham grotto—

> Let such, such only tread this sacred floor,
> Who dare to love their country, and be poor,

we have the feeling that Pope is merely posturing, that he has not come to close quarters with the ideas hypostatised in the words that fall so neatly from his pen.

But we have no such doubt about the satiric poems; there he means what he says, and says it with the most perfect point and finish. Now, satire is not a poetic subject, because it gluts a malevolent emotion. Malevolence, it may be truly urged, really underlies the sublime and every other variety of the literary quality called strength; but in poetry the emotion is subdued, restrained, and garnished, whereas in satire it openly flaunts itself. Yet, if we can detach ourselves from sympathy with the victim, we may admire the brilliance and the art of the onset.

The masterly lines on Addison are in point. No one can help admiring the keenness and skill of the satire, the deadly rapidity of every thrust, the fine art with which Pope admits Addison's virtues, and thus emphasises the exposure of his shortcomings. And this admiration is possible both to those that see in Addison a calm, immaculate figure, intangible by any venom, and to those that maintain the real malice of Thackeray's kindly, genial humourist. But Pope's attack is not always made in the same way. At times it has the cold self-possession of the Addison passage; at times it is more eager, as in the famous portrait of Sporus; at times it takes the form of unrestrained coarseness, as in parts of the *Dunciad*. There are, indeed, passages in the *Dunciad* where Pope seems to grasp with both hands the filth of the streets and hurl it at the votaries of Dulness. But whatever form the attack may take, it is always strong, effective, and finished, even though the reader may regret

>in amber to observe the forms
>Of hairs, or straws, or dirt, or grubs, or worms.

Pope's claim to poetic rank lies, then, in the excellence of his form. We can produce passages, like that on Buckingham in the third Moral Essay, which possess intrinsic poetic merit, but they are not numerous;

while we can produce passage after passage where the splendid workmanship proclaims the artist and provokes admiration. In what has already been said I have drawn attention to the characteristics of Pope's technique—a technique so admirable in its kind that to refuse to admire it is wantonly to limit the area of artistic pleasure. Nor, although its excellences are so pronounced, is it to be sneered at as mechanical.

Mr. Leslie Stephen reminds us that imitation of Pope has not won Pope's immortality; it is easy to reproduce the externals of Pope's manner, but not that quality 'beyond the reach of art' which individualises Pope and eludes appropriation. The compactness and the point of Pope's best work are as far beyond imitation as they are beyond praise. His constant straining after language effects is usually guided by sound taste; he noticeably avoids the circumlocution dear to literary artists like Virgil and Tennyson, and he walks surefootedly among the snares of false antithesis. Now and then he makes a slip. *Windsor Forest* contains this couplet:

> To plains with well-breathed beagles we repair,
> And *trace the mazes of the circling hare.*

The ludicrous loftiness of the second line is a familiar mannerism of Virgil and Tennyson. Does Virgil wish to describe the simple operation of striking fire from flint? He does so thus:

> quærit pars semina flammæ
> Abstrusa in venis silicis.
> Some seek the fiery sparkles sown
> Deep in the veins of cold flint stone.

And Tennyson refers to Arthur's moustache as

> The knightly growth that fringed his lips.

These periphrases are bad, because they lack reality; their deficiency reveals itself at once if they are compared with a just circumlocution, like Milton's:

> Nine times the space that measures day and night
> To mortal men.

The *Ode on Solitude*, a juvenile performance, contains a comical antithesis:

> Whose trees in *summer* yield him *shade*,
> In *winter fire;*

while the *Essay on Man*, one of the maturer compositions, has this line:

> As full, as perfect, in a *hair* as *heart!*

This rivals Tennyson's famous lines on Lord Stratford de Redcliffe:

> Here *silent* in our Minster of the *West*,
> Who wert *the voice* of England in the *East!*

In this way one might go on to point out defects in art, in grammar, in logic, for the purpose of qualifying Pope's excellence, even in the sphere within which he confined himself; but all that could be said in this way would not seriously affect Pope. I prefer to conclude with two reasons why Pope cannot be regarded as a great poet.

The first is, he lacks sincerity. This has already been referred to; but I give one or two additional examples. For the sake of comparison I begin with a little extract where the feeling is genuine:

> Me let the tender office long engage
> To rock the cradle of declining age,
> With lenient arts extend a mother's breath,
> Make languor smile and smooth the bed of death;
> Explore the thought, explain the asking eye,
> And keep awhile one parent from the sky

But the *Messiah* is pure rhetoric·

> No more shall nation against nation rise,
> Nor ardent warriors meet with hateful eyes,

> Nor fields with gleaming steel be cover'd o'er,
> The brazen trumpets kindle rage no more;
> But useless lances into scythes shall bend,
> And the broad falchion in a ploughshare end.

Put over against this the words of the Authorised Version: 'They shall beat their swords into plowshares, and their spears into pruning hooks: nation shall not lift up sword against nation, neither shall they learn war any more.' Or, read the second stanza of the ode in imitation of Hadrian's famous sonnet—

> Hark! they whisper: Angels say,
> Sister spirit, come away.
> What is this absorbs me quite?
> Steals my senses, shuts my sight,
> Drowns my spirit, draws my breath?
> Tell me, my Soul, can this be death?

and then read the corresponding stanza of Bruce's hymn:

> The hour of my departure's come:
> I hear the voice that calls me home:
> At last, O Lord! let trouble cease,
> And let Thy servant die in peace.

The contrast is very striking, the contrast between fine writing and sincere writing. Now, a fatal defect in Pope is that he is too much of a fine writer; he lacks sincerity. A second defect is his want of suggestiveness. Pope's lines are self-contained, whereas the best poetry depends on the reader for its best effect; it comes 'trailing clouds of glory.' No one can miss the point of Pope's couplet—

> While pensive poets painful vigils keep,
> Sleepless themselves, to give their readers sleep;

but the reader must have something of Tennyson's own feeling if he is to realise the magnificent line in *Guinevere*,

> Through the thick night I hear the trumpet blow.

But, if we are content to take what Pope has to offer us, he yields very real and highly artistic pleasure, not, it is true, the pleasure proper to noble poetry, the pleasure of high writing and high thinking; the pleasure, rather, of language perfect after its kind, of language so brilliant that it adorns the stalest commonplace:

> What oft was thought, but ne'er so well expressed.

Emily Brontë

EMILY BRONTË

WHEN Mrs. Gaskell wrote her *Life of Charlotte Brontë*, general opinion justified her, as it would still justify her, in regarding Charlotte as undoubtedly the most gifted of the three sisters—Charlotte, Emily, and Anne Brontë. But the position thus assigned by the many to the elder sister has not been approved by the critics, and would not have been accepted by Charlotte herself, who was fully alive to Emily's extraordinary powers, and keenly sensitive to any recognition of them. Of Emily she writes that 'under an unsophisticated culture, inartificial tastes, and an unpretending outside lay a secret power and fire that might have informed the brain and kindled the veins of a hero,' and a regret ever with her was that, with rare exceptions, critics failed to recognise the greatness that Emily revealed in the few compositions swift-coming death permitted. With eager gratitude, therefore, did she accept Sydney Dobell's praise of *Wuthering Heights*. It cheered and revived her, although by the time the words were written Emily was 'chill to praise or blame.' She would have rejoiced greatly if she could have so forecast the years as to know what of praise for Emily the future held in store.

In emphatic language Mr. Swinburne has declared that Charlotte and Emily Brontë and Mrs. Browning make up 'the perfect trinity for England of highest female fame.' Mr. Bayne pronounces Emily Brontë 'one of the most extraordinary women that ever lived,' and adds that 'many grounds might be shown for believing her genius more powerful, her promise more rich than those of her sister Charlotte.' His examination of the poems written by the three sisters leads him to a conclusion proclaimed by Charlotte herself, and now accepted by competent critics, that Emily's are beyond measure the best. In his *Life of Charlotte Brontë* Mr. Wemyss Reid passes the same judgment on Emily's poetry, while its absolute merits are attested by its finding a place in Ward's anthology of English verse.

Charlotte Brontë would have joyed over such testimony to her sister's kinship with 'the breed of noble bloods.'

Emily Brontë was born at Hartshead-cum-Clifton, near Leeds, in 1818. In 1820 her father removed to Haworth, and in the parsonage there Emily spent nearly her whole life. Mrs. Gaskell has used all her artistic skill to deepen the impression of the gloom that hung over Haworth parsonage. In the opening chapter of the life, as she takes her reader with her on the way from Keighley to Haworth, she is careful to strike the key-note of the composition—a note of utter sadness.

The neighbourhood of Haworth is so described as to induce a feeling of depression that never leaves the reader. The picture of Haworth parsonage confirms the mournful impression made by the landscape. That cold, grey house, overlooking the terribly crowded churchyard, seems a fit habitation for the nervous, timid woman Mrs. Gaskell presents to us as Charlotte Brontë—a woman suffering from ill-health, troubled by depression of spirits, haunted by superstitious fancies—all aggravated by the intolerable burden of her unhappy brother's misdoings; but this is not the

Charlotte Brontë of her novels—the fastidious, painstaking artist, the fearless, self-reliant woman.

At the same time the story of the Brontë family *is* full of a pathos not to be mitigated by any merely human consolations. The three sisters passed through a motherless childhood, uncheered by any large amount of kindly sympathy. Their father, to whom they might naturally have looked for some compensation for their great loss, was a cold, selfish man, who, even in his wife's lifetime, took his meals apart from his family. Their aunt, who came to Haworth after Mrs. Brontë died, did her duty nobly, as far as concerned everything connected with housekeeping; but she had no power of entering into or even conceiving the workings of the active minds around her. Tabby, the faithful servant, was probably the most appreciative and sympathetic of the grown-up people in that Yorkshire parsonage. And so the girls grew to womanhood, drawn ever nearer to each other by similarity of pursuits and aspirations, and by a strong family affection.

The shattering of the family circle was terribly sudden and complete. Their brother

Patrick, whose conduct had so disgraced and pained his friends and relatives, died in September, 1848, Emily in December of the same year, Anne in May, 1849. Thus, in the short space of eight months Charlotte Brontë was left the sole survivor of the Brontë family, the lonely occupant of the room where in days gone by she and her sisters, their duties done, discussed their plans and ambitions, as they paced backwards and forwards in the flickering firelight. Only a few short years were to pass before Charlotte herself was called away, and laid

> By the lone church that stands amid the moors.

Yet it was not always winter on these sweeping moors. The girlhood of the three sisters was not without happiness—quiet, doubtless, but real and wholesome. They found deep joy in the moors; they loved them when the snow lay deep, and the winter winds rushed from the hills; they loved them when the kindly warmth of summer lured out blossoms; they loved them most of all when autumn brought the dusky glow of the heather. Their affection for each other was a source of intense happiness; it proved, indeed, a source of deep anguish when first Emily and then Anne was wrapped from loving eyes in death's chill mist; but not death itself could destroy the memory of loving intercourse. Their intellectual pursuits were another source of delight: they found real and abiding pleasure in writing their poems and novels, and in discussing with each other the subjects and the plans of their compositions.

Emily's earliest education was got at home from her aunt, Miss Branwell, and from her father. Miss Branwell was an excellent housekeeper, and she succeeded in passing on her skill to her nieces. Charlotte Brontë and her friend Harriet Martineau refute the popular generalisation that intellectual women are poor housekeepers. Every woman that strays beyond the limits of housewifery is not necessarily a Mrs. Jellyby. The Rev. Patrick Brontë gave his children lessons, and at the same time looked after their physical well-being according to principles strictly Spartan. Not least important, as a mind-forming influence, were the amusements of these precocious children. From a very eary age they read indiscriminately, wrote, and got up plays; the interaction of minds so keen and so early active was bound to be highly formative. Of school education Emily had exceedingly little. Her home yearning was such that frequent or prolonged absence from Haworth was a physical impossibility—only on the open, breezy Yorkshire moors could her wild spirit find a congenial atmosphere. Charlotte has told what an effort it cost Emily to spend some time with her at a Continental school. 'She was never happy till she carried her hard-won knowledge back to the remote English village, the old parsonage house, and desolate Yorkshire hills.' The records of her school-days testify to her strength of intellect, her stubborn tenacity of will, her strong, wild imagination. The Brussels visit was her last absence from the parsonage. The few years that remained were spent quietly at home, for a private school scheme long cherished by the sisters never came to anything. Her last days have been described by her elder sister in words that reveal to us her stern, unbending character. A notable fact not, however, recorded by Charlotte is that, like her brother, Emily died standing.

Emily Brontë is described as having had, like Charlotte, a bad complexion; but she was tall and well-formed, while her eyes were of remarkable beauty. Her mental gifts were of a high order. In spite of her imperfect culture this is abundantly proved by her writings, few as they are. Her temperament was such that to strangers she rarely if ever unbent, while even her own relatives stood in some awe of her. At the same time she was capable of strong affection. She was deeply attached to her sisters, and passionately fond of dumb animals, insects, and flowers.

As might be supposed, Emily did not favourably impress outsiders. Mrs. Gaskell says that all she could learn about Emily tended to give an unpleasant impression of her; but, as she properly points out, Emily has been portrayed for us in *Shirley*, by her sister Charlotte, who knew her as no stranger could ever have known her. In Shirley's character we find not only such traits as other observers have noted in Emily's, but also characteristics hid from the outer world —joyousness of heart, kindly, womanly sympathy, warm, deep emotions.

From the sketch given of Emily Brontë's life, one can readily see that she could have owed little to influences outside Haworth and little more to reading; for, situated as she was, she could have had access to only a comparatively small number of books. The question then is, whence came the influences that helped to form the powerful character that confronts us in her writings? One potent influence was the moors. They were to her more than objects of sensuous enjoyment. She loved them with a deep, passionate love: they informed her with their own strong, wild nature; their dreariest, gloomiest aspects found harmonies in her stern spirit; their purple heather glowing in the autumn sun stirred her with full, rich joy.

Charlotte has written of her sister's love for the moors, and in Emily's novel, *Wuthering Heights*, a striking passage reveals the pleasure Emily derived from the scenery about Haworth. 'He said the pleasantest manner of spending a hot July day was lying from morning till evening on a bank of heath in the middle of the moors, with the bees humming dreamily about among the bloom, and the larks singing high up overhead, and the blue sky and bright sun shining steadily and cloudlessly. That was his most perfect ideal of heaven's happiness; mine was rocking in a rustling green tree, with a west wind blowing and bright white clouds flitting rapidly above, and not only larks, but throstles, and blackbirds, and linnets, and cuckoos, pouring out music on every side, and the moors seen at a distance, broken into cool, dusky dells; but close by great swells of long grass undulating in waves to the breezes, and woods and sounding water, and the whole world awake and wild with joy.' The same feeling finds expression in her poems, as in *The Blubell*, and in the piece beginning, 'Loud without the wind was roaring.'

Another powerful influence was her father. He is described as a passionate, self-willed, vain, cold, and distant man, stern and determined, ever eager to maintain his opinions, whether or not they harmonised with the popular judgment—a man, indeed, whose instincts were soldierly rather than priestly. This description is so far supported by Charlotte's presentment of him in the Mr. Helstone of *Shirley*. Mr. Brontë had many wild stories and traditions of his native Ireland, and he delighted, by means of them, to excite terror in his children. We may be sure that, despite their terrifying effect, these tales of danger and dread appealed strongly to Emily's bold and fearless mind.

Similar stories were told to the children by their aunt, Miss Branwell, who had brought from Cornwall a goodly store of such weird narratives as Mr. Hunt has brought together in his *Romances and Drolls of the West of England.* Tabby was an authority on Yorkshire traditions, and had strange things to tell of old-world doings in the county. The effect of all this was early seen. While still in the nursery the little Brontës were writing romances, and all Emily's stories reflected the wild, creepy tales she had become familiar with.

On a larger scale the same influence is at work in Emily's extraordinary novel *Wuthering Heights.* For extraordinary it is, whether we regard the form or the substance. There are faults of expression and of treatment; but in *Wuthering Heights* we have the first novel of a young woman with little knowledge either of literature or of life, and yet the story is told with compactness and force, scenery is described with marvellous vividness and sympathy, characters are represented with amazing individuality, while, though incidents and characters are at times so appalling that many readers turn from the book in horror, there is such power, both of personality and of treatment, as positively fascinates even while it terrifies.

But it should be noted Emily Brontë had no conscious intention of exciting terror. It is true that, as Heathcliff reveals himself in all his savagery, one stands aghast at his wolfish ferocity; yet one can plainly see that the author is not seeking for means of affecting her readers, but, heedless of readers, is working out her altogether astounding conception.

The promise of the book is found not in the story (though what story there is is clearly told) but in the delineation of character. Heathcliff is a wonderful, if repulsive, creation. His wife asks questions that the reader often asks: 'Is Mr. Heathcliff a man? If so, is he mad? And, if not, is he a devil?' It is difficult to say when he is most terrible—when he is behaving like the incarnation of cruelty, when he is raving in the very delirium of passionate love for Catherine Earnshaw, when he is wandering by midnight among the graves out on the moors, haunted by a feeling of the presence of the dead Catherine, when he is calling on her spirit with wailings of intensest agony, or when in the last days he moves like one in a dream, seeing some vision that gladdens him and yet robs him of all power to live, till the morning comes when he is found dead, with fierce and staring eyes. A repulsive creation, and yet it may safely be said that the imagination that conjured up a monster like Heathcliff, and developed his character with such force, was equal to high creative work.

But there is more than potential merit of character-drawing. The younger Catherine has some charming traits: her light-heartedness and fearlessness, if at times they seem to verge on recklessness and careless despair, are at other times exceedingly attractive. Isabella Linton, though an inconsistent and somewhat sketchy conception, shows glimpses of a noble dignity when face to face with the dreadful life she has to lead at *Wuthering Heights*. Edgar Linton, if cast in too weak a mould, is yet in many respects well drawn. Gentleness, courtesy, deep and true affection, and scholarly tastes, make him a strong contrast to the wild and uncultured Heathcliff, that 'arid wilderness of furze and whinstone'; and if at times his character is allowed to become ignobly unmanly, enough of excellence remains to show that Emily Brontë could conceive a refined and cultured mind.

Probably the strongest assurance that her genius was capable of careful, steady work as well as of wild flights is to be found in the two servants, Nelly Dean and Joseph. Both characters are well conceived, but Joseph is admirable. His faithfulness to the family he had served so long, his rugged nature, his unbending and repellent Calvinism, his certainty as to his own sanctity and his doubt as to every other body's—all these are well set forth. Joseph is interesting in another way: he gives Emily Brontë opportunities of showing that she can handle the ludicrous with considerable effect. There is genuine humour in some of Joseph's appearances, all the more that his efforts as a humorist are quite unconscious.

In strong contrast to the gloom cast over the story by Heathcliff is the beauty of those passages that tell how Catherine Linton does all she can to soften the ruggedness in Hareton Earnshaw's disposition, and to raise him above the degraded level to which Heathcliff had depressed him, and of those that reveal the author's susceptibility to nature under all aspects. She is alive to the beauty of darkening moors and bright blue skies, of bare hillside and wooded valley, of carolling birds and whispering trees and murmuring streams. Her love of nature carries her into veins of thought that recall the imaginings of Shelley. Lockwood had gone to visit the lonely churchyard where lay Heathcliff, Edgar Linton, and Catherine Earnshaw, and he thus concludes the story of *Wuthering Heights*: 'I lingered round them under that benign sky; watched the moths fluttering among the heath and harebells, listened to the soft wind breathing through the grass, and wondered how anyone could ever imagine unquiet slumbers for sleepers in that quiet earth.'

Charlotte Brontë compares her sister's novel to a figure rudely carved from a granite block: 'There it stands, colossal, dark, and frowning —half statue, half rock; in the former sense terrible and goblin-like, in the latter almost beautiful, for its colouring is of mellow grey, and moorland moss clothes it, and heath, with its blooming bells and balmy fragrance, grows faithfully close to the giant's foot.' Rude *Wuthering Heights* is, but it *has* power and it *has* beauty, and when its author died our literature lost a novelist of great promise.

Emily Brontë's poetry is equally full of power, but it is perhaps equally unlikely to find readers. This is not because of anything in it so repellent as what is to be found in *Wuthering Heights*. On the contrary, its feeling for nature, its pensiveness, above all the grandeur of thought and the strength of soul in the finest passages, are in themselves attractive. The fatal defect is the want of form; only now and again is the expression worthy of the conception. Something, too, might be said against a certain gloom in the poems, due to their renunciation of hope and love and joy, were this not fully redeemed by their passion for nature and their lofty resolution. If joy leaves us, never to return, we are not to despair.

> There should be no despair for you
>   While nightly stars are burning;
> While evening pours its silent dew,
>   And sunshine gilds the morning.

> There should be no despair—though tears
>   May flow down like a river:
> Are not the best beloved of years
>   Around your heart for ever?
> They weep, you weep, it must be so,
>   Winds sigh as you are sighing,
> And Winter sheds its grief in snow
>   Where Autumn's leaves are lying:
> Yet, these revive, and from their fate,
>   Your fate cannot be parted:
> Then, journey on, if not elate,
>   Still *never* broken-hearted!

Of Emily Brontë it may be truly said she was never broken-hearted. Even sorrow and deadly sickness could not subdue the unbending firmness of her soul. When death was coming very near, she wrote in her wonderful last lines:

> O God within my breast,
> Almighty, ever-present Deity!
>   Life—that in me has rest,
> As I—undying Life—have power in thee!
>   . . . . .
>   There is no room for Death,
> Nor atom that his might could render void:
>   Thou—Thou art Being and Breath,
> And what Thou art may never be destroyed.

Here is what supremely fascinates the admirers of Emily Brontë's poems—the brave, strong spirit that, even when cabined and confined by conventional verse-forms, flames and dances in its bounds.

> I'll walk where my own nature would be leading;
> It vexes me to choose another guide,

she cries in proud independence, and echoes the prayer of *The Old Stoic*:

> Riches I hold in light esteem,
>   And Love I laugh to scorn;
> And lust of fame was but a dream,
>   That vanished with the morn:
> And if I pray, the only prayer
>   That moves my lips for me
> Is, Leave the heart that now I bear,
>   And give me liberty!
> Yes, as my swift days near their goal,
>   'Tis all that I implore;
> In life and death a chainless soul,
>   With courage to endure.

In this there is the very abandon of self-reliance, the uncontrolled utterance of fearlessness.

The softer qualities of the poems are seen in compositions like *Remembrance* (though it contains a characteristic note of strength), *The Outcast Mother, A Death Scene, The Wanderer from the Fold*. What the author had achieved in the way of pure melody is fairly represented in these lines:

> Blow, west wind, by the lonely mound,
>   And murmur, summer streams—
> There is no need of other sound
>   To soothe my lady's dreams.

Careful reading of Emily Brontë's poetry deepens the regret that, after perusing *Wuthering Heights*, one feels for her early death. She passed away before her rare powers had time fully to reveal themselves though not before she had written enough to indicate the richness of her promise. How rich was not recognised in her lifetime, though of this she never complained. She complained, indeed, of nothing. Yet appreciation would doubtless have given her pleasure, self-controlled and self-reliant as she was. Praise of the highest kind has been freely bestowed on her work, but too late to gratify her, for, in her own fine words:

> The dweller in the land of death
>   Is changed and careless too.

Some Characteristics of Scott's Poetry

SOME CHARACTERISTICS OF SCOTT'S POETRY

To those interested in sound literature, and more especially in the pure, wholesome literature with which Scott enriched British poetry, it is matter of hearty satisfaction to note how persistently, despite all fluctuations in taste whatsoever, taste individual, or taste periodic, Scott's poetry asserts its claims to attention, and the present time is not inopportune for re-stating some of the excellences of Scott's work in verse, for once more his poetic masterpieces are high in the favour of the general reader.

Accepting Matthew Arnold's three-fold estimate of the literary genius, I propose to show that the critical estimate combines with the personal and the historic to assign a high place among the poets to Sir Walter Scott.

And first, then, of the personal in his poetry, of what attracts us because it appeals to our heart, and of what pleases us because it seems to reflect the manly and honourable character of Scott himself.

Scott wins us by his sympathetic description of our native land, by his reproduction in verse of that scenery amid which we were reared, love of which is bound up with our very being, the memory of which saddens the exile in the fairest of foreign lands. Bare and rugged our birth-place may be, yet the tropics in all their glory never displace from the heart of our countrymen the

> Land of brown heath and shaggy wood,
> Land of the mountain and the flood.

One of Beattie's most eloquent passages dwells on the lonely melancholy of the Highlands, their mountain deserts, their sparsely-peopled valleys; but this land has entwined itself with the very heartstrings of its people, and Scott has finely expressed their admiration and their love.

> Farewell to each cliff, on which breakers are foaming;
> Farewell, each dark glen, in which red deer are roaming;

> Farewell, lonely Skye, to lake, mountain, and river;
> Macleod may return, but Mackrimmon shall never!
>
> Too oft shall the notes of Mackrimmon's bewailing
> Be heard when the Gael on their exile are sailing;
> Dear land! to the shores whence unwilling we sever,
> Return—return—return shall we never.

The distinctive features in one of the finest of Highland landscapes are portrayed in the view that charms the eye of Fitz-James when he has toiled up the far projecting precipice, and

> One burnish'd sheet of living gold,
> Loch Katrine lay beneath him roll'd.

Not less effective is the picture of barren desolation in *The Lord of the Isles*, where

> All is rocks at random thrown,
> Black waves, bare crags, and banks of stone.

The same poem is adorned with some striking passages descriptive of the wild waters that break on our western shores. The stanzas that describe the approach of Bruce's bark to the Castle of Artornish are in Scott's finest vein.

But his Muse has hung even more fondly over that border district which is peculiarly Scott-land. No one can wander by Yarrow and Ettrick and Tweed, by fair Melrose and the mystic Eildons, without feeling haunted by the very presence of Scott. As the happy pilgrim roams in the border country, and views grey scaur and shining stream, thought is ever with him that loved them well, and drew from them the inspiration of undying verse. We linger fondly over the many tributes Scott pays to the charms of our native land—the moonlight beauty of Melrose, the quiet peace of Yarrow, the romantic fascination of Ettrick Forest, of Tweed and Teviot, of bare hill and lonesome valley. And Scott has added to our life a deep and abiding pleasure by rooting firmly in us the tradition and history of our country. We owe it to him that no walk in almost any part of Scotland need be solitary; he has peopled every crumbling keep and ruined abbey, every hillside and solitary glen; priest and warrior, wizard and bard, courtly scholar and wild borderer, give life and interest to every decaying memorial of the past; while in the breeze that sighs among the loneliest hills we seem to hear the Spirit of the Flood whispering to the Spirit of the Fell.

But this warm love for 'Caledonia stern and

wild' is only one form of Scott's patriotism. The land itself is so dear to him that one of his strongest passages is inspired by contempt for him

> Whose heart hath ne'er within him burn'd,
> As home his footsteps he hath turn'd
> From wandering on a foreign strand.

But equally dear to him is all that concerns the history of Scotland and the part played by Scotland in British history. Some of the best and most highly finished of Scott's poetry poured from him when Britain was in the throes of her desperate struggle with the first Napoleon, such as the fine lines on Nelson and on Pitt. A still stronger feeling runs through passages where Scots valour is the theme, as in *Don Roderick*, where Scott dwells on the desperate courage of the Highland regiments, and yet more notably in the descriptions of Bannockburn and Flodden.

Scott also appeals to us by the romantic tone of his verse. The primary emotions are pre-eminently susceptible, and the poet is ever sure of an audience when he sings of adventures by flood and field, of love and war, of wrong defeated and right triumphant. The interest of these themes is prominent in

Scott's poetry, and is sustained by the quick movement and the gay colour of the language. Nor are Scott's tones of pathos less responsive to human cravings. Laments over the decay of Nature and humanity, the death of bright hopes and the shattering of fair visions, find an echo in every heart. And we often hear these notes of sadness thrilling from the Harp of the North.

Not less attractive is the fine, wholesome tone that marks all Scott's writings, both his prose and his poetry. Scott was one of the most modest of men, and at a time when practically the whole civilised world was moved by his writings, he steadfastly depreciated his work and deprecated the adulation so freely offered to him. Yet, as his life advanced and he looked back on his literary labours, he justly congratulated himself on the pleasure he had given to thousands of his fellow-creatures and on the purity of his writing. In his interesting reminiscences of St. Andrews, Dr. Boyd tells that he met the late Mr. Trollope at dinner, and that in the course of conversation the popular novelist rather pooh-poohed the Waverley novels, and took it upon himself to question whether if they had appeared in our time they would have made such a mark. The observation was, of course, a silly one, because, if Scott had written in our day, he might not perhaps have written exactly as he did, but he would still have written like Scott. But waiving that, how great the relief to turn from the sickly introspection and the analysis of the garbage of human nature so frequent now to the fresh, wholesome fiction of the Waverley novels. And the poems are equally manly. Scott does not shirk dealing with the sexual relation, but his treatment is utterly free from prurience: he accepts it as one among many human relations; he does not, after the manner of some modern writers, flaunt it in our face as if it monopolised human nature. And the result is that, while his writings lose nothing in breadth of treatment, they are pre-eminently fresh and wholesome.

I would remark in the last place with regard to the personal estimate of Scott, that we like the poems because they reveal to us a fine character. The autobiography found in the introductory epistles to *Marmion* and in the reflective passages scattered through the poems, strengthens the impression made on us by the poetry as a whole, that Scott was an attractive personality. And those that admire Scott have the satisfaction of knowing that the more they get to learn about Scott the more are their admiration and liking increased. Recent Scott publications have assured us that the qualities we have learned to esteem in the poems, in the novels, in *Lockhart's Life*, were fundamental parts of Scott's character. The *Journal* and the *Familiar Letters* have admitted us to very close intimacy with Scott, and this intimacy has served only to increase our liking for him and to strengthen his hold on us.

I pass now to consider how Scott is affected by the historic estimate. He rode high on that great wave of poetry which, towards the close of the eighteenth century, overwhelmed the feeble conventionality that marked the decay of the classical school. Pope himself is conventional, but in his hands the close-knit heroic couplet, sparkling with all the artifices of rhetoric, is an attractive form of verse, while his want of close contact with and of immediate response to nature, is so far counterbalanced by his sonorous eloquence, his polished didactic, his brilliant and piercing satire. Moreover, Pope's writing is stamped with an impressive individuality which long dominated the poetic field, yielding somewhat to poets like Gray and Collins, but compelling the majority—even men like Johnson and Goldsmith—to adopt the Pope manner. Of course, such writers as Johnson and Goldsmith preserved a measure of independence, but as the century grew old poetry fell on evil days; it preserved merely the form without the substance. It was of this time that Lloyd wrote:

> Tale, elegy, or lofty ode,
> We travel on the beaten road.

Nor did those of the old school that left the beaten road walk in the path that led up Parnassus. Erasmus Darwin certainly succeeded in finding new didactic on which to employ Pope's verse, but it is difficult to poetise such subjects as the thesis that manures are to vegetables as chyle is to animals. Darwin's *Botanic Garden* appeared in 1791; Scott's translation of *Bürger's Ballads* appeared in 1796, and contains verse like this:

> Tramp! tramp! along the land they rode,
> Splash! splash! along the sea,
> The scourge is red, the spur drops blood,
> The flashing pebbles flee.

This is rather different from Darwin's exposition of the resemblance between manure and chyle, and it is worth while to ask how such verse as this of Scott's came to the front.

During the reign of the classical school there were stirrings of a freer music and a more natural poetry, while from time to time new influences affected the course of literature. Thomson, Collins, Gray, and Goldsmith testify by manner and matter to the existence within the classical school of natural verse; yet, by a certain coldness, or by a certain inaptness of phraseology, they suggest the unpoetic atmosphere in which they lived. Contemporary with Gray and Goldsmith was Chatterton, and in his verse we find that same influence which in later days revived and invigorated poetry. Meantime literature was slowly absorbing influences antagonistic to the classical school. In 1765 Percy published his *Reliques of Ancient English Poetry*, a book that did much to help the growth of more natural poetry. In the preceding year Grainger had published a poetic account of the culture of the sugar-cane, and, in the most approved classical fashion, had refined the negroes by calling them swains! What a relief for the readers of the day to open *Percy's Reliques* and light upon verse like this:

> O Nancy, wilt thou go with me,
>   Nor sigh to leave the flaunting town?
> Can silent glens have charms for thee,
>   The lonely cot and russet gown?
> No longer dressed in silken sheen,
>   No longer decked with jewels rare,
> Say, canst thou quit each courtly scene,
>   Where thou wert fairest of the fair?

German poetry co-operated with early English poetry to shake the hold of the classical school. In translating German poetry and thus bringing its influence to bear on English literature, a prominent part was taken by William Taylor of Norwich, whose example, indeed, it was that stimulated Scott to similar attempts. Another conspicuous illustration of the German influence is Coleridge. A wide gulf separates the eighteenth century treatment of the pagan gods from that we find in Coleridge's imitation of Schiller:

> Never, believe me,
> Appear the Immortals,
> Never alone:
> Scarce had I welcomed the Sorrow-beguiler,
> Iacchus! but in came Boy Cupid the Smiler:
> Lo! Phœbus the Glorious descends from his throne!

> They advance, they float in, the Olympians all!
>   With Divinities fills my
>   Terrestrial hall!

Though it may sound paradoxical, classical influence also contributed to the overthrow of the classical school. Classicality to an eighteenth-century poet referred mainly to form; it demanded polish and compression. But Greek poetry is distinguished by more than by excellence of form; it is equally noteworthy for its open-eyedness to beauty, for its exaltation of the delight of mere existence. Shelley and Keats reflect to us these characteristics of the classical spirit. Last and chiefest among the potencies that enveloped literature in the closing years of the last century is the French Revolution, that terrible protest against unreality and convention, that fierce demand for a return to nature. Poets responded at once to the cry of the Revolutionaries for liberty, equality, fraternity. The intense fervour with which the Revolution filled the hearts of mankind had a profound effect on literature. In our own country poetry rose to a level of magnificence that recalls

>   those melodious bursts that fill
> The spacious times of great Elizabeth
>   With sounds that echo still.

As the conjoint result of the various influences I have referred to, poetry became more real; it went to nature for its material and brought that material to bear directly on its readers; it became charged with higher beauty, with nobler sentiments, with loftier thoughts; it spoke with more varied expression, in tones more richly musical. Let us select a few lines from Pope:

> See how the world its veterans rewards!
> A youth of frolics, an old age of cards;
> Fair to no purpose, artful to no end,
> Young without lovers, old without a friend:
> A fop their passion, but their prize a sot;
> Alive, ridiculous, and dead, forgot!

These lines are the perfection of brief, pointed expression, but compare them as poetry with the opening of *Kubla Khan*.

> In Xanadu did Kubla Khan
> A stately pleasure-dome decree:
> Where Alph, the sacred river ran,
> Through caverns measureless to man,
> Down to a sunless sea.

It was then in such an age of true poetry that Scott wrote; he has the importance that belongs to the leaders of great literary movements; all his poetry is instinct with that love of nature, that romantic spirit, that fiery glow, that swift movement, that warm patriotism which give life and distinction to the poetry of his time. We know how eagerly his great poems were read, how thoroughly they harmonised with the spirit of the age. A striking passage in Lockhart's *Life* tells how well Scott's verse suited that time of high endeavour—'In the course of the day, when *The Lady of the Lake* first reached Sir Adam Fergusson, he was posted with his company on a point of ground exposed to the enemy's artillery, somewhere, no doubt, on the lines of Torres Vedras. The men were ordered to lie prostrate on the ground; while they kept that attitude, the captain, kneeling at the head, read aloud the description of the battle in canto vi., and the listening soldiers only interrupted him by a joyous huzza when the French shot struck the bank close above them.' And thus we find that the historic estimate unites with the personal to make Scott a conspicuous figure in literature.

It remains to test him by the impartial estimate, to ascertain his intrinsic claim to admiration. For there is the undoubted fact that Scott has kept a firm hold on lovers of poetry, on readers of a critical disposition, as well as on readers less exacting, on readers to whom his Scots characteristics do not specially appeal, as well as on readers to whom his strong national tone endears him, on readers abroad as well as on readers at home. And we have to explain this, or at least to try to understand on what Scott relied when he produced the poems that, though largely indebted to adventitious circumstances for their original and enduring reputation, have nevertheless won the praise of those with whom these adventitious circumstances count for very little.

A prominent feature of Scott's verse is its swift and exhilarating movement His lines have the ring of popular verse, of verse that pleases the ordinary reader of poetry, and is relished by the fastidious and critical. We do not need to be told that the popular ear was caught by verse like this:

> Scarce could they hear, or see their foes,
> Until at weapon point they close.
> They close in clouds of smoke and dust,
> With sword-sway and with lance's thrust;
>   And such a yell was there
> Of sudden and portentous birth,
> As if men fought upon the earth,
>   And fiends in upper air;

> Oh! life and death were in the shout,
> Recoil and rally, charge and rout,
>   And triumph and despair.

But this is not only popular verse—the verse of the average man. We know that a poet like Campbell, who preserved to a romantic age the fastidious refinement of the classical school, was carried away by the vivacity of Scott's movement. Campbell was especially impressed by that fine ballad, *Cadzow Castle*.

> Mightiest of all the beasts of chase
>   That roam in woody Caledon,
> Crashing the forest in his race,
>   The mountain bull comes thundering on.
>
> Fierce on the hunter's quivered band
>   He rolls his eyes of swarthy glow,
> Spurns with black hoof and horn the sand,
>   And tosses high his mane of snow.

We find this stimulating and attractive characteristic in Scott's lines whatever form of versification he may adopt. This 'hurried frankness,' as Scott himself calls it, overcomes the monotony inherent in perfectly regular composition.

> The Saxons shout, their mate to cheer,
> The helpless females scream for fear,

And yells for rage the mountaineer.
'Twas then, as by the outcry riven,
Pour'd down at once the lowering heaven:
A whirlwind swept Loch Katrine's breast,
Her billows rear'd their snowy crest.
Well for the swimmer swell'd they high
To mar the Highland marksman's eye;
For round him shower'd, 'mid rain and hail,
The vengeful arrows of the Gael.

A second characteristic of Scott's poetry is its simplicity; its full force is felt at once. No mental power is consumed in wrestling with the meaning or in realising a complicated group of circumstances, and hence the emotional effect is the greatest possible. Scott's simplicity is pervasive, and admits of ample and varied illustration. I shall content myself with directing attention to one or two varieties of this quality. And first I would remark that Scott, when he wishes to use illustrative language, avails himself of easy and familiar figures. He does not attempt, as Tennyson does, to seek novelty by introducing unwontedly familiar or out-of-the-way comparisons. His figures, however, have the merit of being distinctly impressive; their simplicity does not mar the effect. A few examples will illustrate this.

'Thanks, noble Surrey!' Marmion said,
Nor farther greeting there he paid;
But, parting like a thunderbolt,
First in the vanguard made a halt.

Then mark'd they, dashing broad and far,
The broken billows of the war,
And plumèd crests of chieftains brave,
Floating like foam upon the wave.

Spears shook, and falchions flash'd amain;
Fell England's arrow-flight like rain.

The fiery youth, with desperate charge,
Made, for a space, an opening large,—
  The rescued banner rose,—
But darkly closed the war around;
Like pine tree, rooted from the ground,
  It sunk among the foes.

But yet, though thick the shafts as snow,
Though charging knights like whirlwinds go,
Though bill-men ply the ghastly blow,
  Unbroken was the ring;
The stubborn spearmen still made good
Their dark impenetrable wood,
Each stepping where his comrade stood,
  The instant that he fell.

How simple all this is, yet how appropriate and effective. It seems very natural to compare Marmion on his swift steed to a thunderbolt, the waving crests of the chiefs to foam on the sea, a flight of arrows to a shower of rain or of snow, a close-set group of spearmen to a dark wood. Yet how impressive these illustrations are, how admirably they suit the feeling of the poetry, and how vividly they bring before our mind the battle scene on that disastrous day at Flodden.

These figures have not the elaboration of Tennyson's description of the fall of the Red Knight, who fell

> As the crest of some slow-arching wave
> Heard in dead night along that table shore,
> Drops flat, and after the great waters break,
> Whitening for half a league, and thin themselves,
> Far over sands marbled with moon and cloud,
> From less and less to nothing.

This careful art is the antithesis of Scott's rapid strokes, and has its own distinctive beauty, but it is not suited to vigorous writing, and as a matter of fact Tennyson's battle scenes make a very poor figure beside Scott's description of Flodden.

The simplicity that we have found in Scott's figures is equally observable in his treatment of the feelings. Read, for example, the description of Oswald's troubled sleep:

> There might be seen of shame the blush,
> There anger's dark and fiercer flush,
> While the perturbed sleeper's hand
> Seem'd grasping dagger-knife, or brand.
> Relax'd that grasp, the heavy sigh,
> The tear in the half-opening eye,
> The pallid cheek and brow confess'd
> That grief was busy in his breast;
> Nor paused that mood—a sudden start
> Impell'd the life-blood from the heart;
> Features convulsed and mutterings dread
> Show terror reigns in sorrow's stead.

We read the successive emotions in their outward expression, and this simple objective method of mental description is characteristic of Scott. There is an excellent example in *Marmion* where the song, 'Where shall the lover rest?' revived Marmion's memory of Constance, and twice he rose to cry 'To horse!' Finer still is the description of the old harper's embarrassment when he is asked to play.

Scott's simplicity of treatment extends to his descriptive passages. Indeed one of his characteristic excellences is the easy grasp he conveys to his readers of whatever scene he undertakes to describe, be it a great castle like Norham Keep, or a stretch of landscape like the view from Blackford Hill. In every case Scott seizes on bold, striking, defining features, and declines to dwell on minor points. It is highly instructive to compare Scott's landscapes with Wordsworth's; in the latter case the poet is sometimes so anxious to include everything that the intellect is strained to conceive the scene, and in consequence some of the poetic effect is missed. Scott never makes this mistake. Take the opening stanzas of *Marmion*:

> Day set on Norham's castled steep,
> And Tweed's fair river, broad and deep,
>   And Cheviot's mountains lone:
> The battled towers, the donjon keep,
> The loophole grates where captives weep,
> The flanking walls that round it sweep
>   In yellow lustre shone.
> The warriors on the turrets high
> Moving athwart the evening sky,
>   Seem'd forms of giant height:
> Their armour, as it caught the rays,
> Flash'd back again the western blaze
>   In lines of dazzling light.

This is admirably done. With one or two strokes Scott paints the surroundings of Norham, the fair shining Tweed, and the lone

Cheviots, and then right in the heart of the picture sets the stately fortress, lit up by the setting sun. Observe how effectively he introduces the yellow lustre of the walls, the warriors high up against the sky, and the flash of their armour. His feeling for these strong descriptive touches is sure and firm, and is abundantly illustrated in *The Lady of the Lake.*

> Each purple peak, each flinty spire,
> Was bathed in floods of living fire.
> But not a setting beam could glow
> Within the dark ravine below.

In the succeeding stanzas the poet makes lavish use of the primrose, the violet, the grey birch, the glistening oak, the blue of heaven, in order to give life and colour to the description. A favourite feature is the red berries of the rowan, which so conspicuously brighten Scottish sylvan scenery.

> How broad the shadows of the oak,
> How clung the rowan to the rock,
> And through the foliage show'd his head,
> With narrow leaves and berries red.

Red, as a strong colour, is often employed by Scott.

> When red hath set the beamless sun
> Through heavy vapours dark and dun.

> When the sun his beacon red
> Had kindled on Benvoirlich's head.

And again in *Rokeby*.

> Thus circled in his coil the snake,
> When roving hunters beat the brake,
> Watches with red and glistening eye.

The last line is a fine stroke. The same poem illustrates Scott's liking for the brightness given to a picture by the sparkle of sun-lit waters. He describes the Greta

> rejoicing free
> As captive set at liberty,
> Flashing her sparkling waves abroad,
> And clamouring joyful on her road.

Scott's love for strong simple effects naturally leads him to employ strong contrasts. I have already illustrated this from *The Lady of the Lake*, in the lines where he paints yellow and purple on a sombre background. A simpler, but not a less strong example is afforded in the famous description of Melrose.

> When the broken arches are black in night,
> And each shafted oriel glimmers white,
> When buttress and buttress alternately
> Seem framed of ebon and ivory.

Scott's descriptions, then, are marked by the selection of strong, striking features, and the neglect of minor points, by the general employment of strong colours and strong contrasts—the result being pictures that are impressive and readily conceived. One of the best illustrations is the description of the view towards Edinburgh from Blackford Hill. Not to dwell on other points in this fine passage, I would lay stress on the strong effect produced by the dusky grandeur of Edinburgh, aglow with gloomy splendour red, against the more brilliantly lighted background, the purple Ochils and the gleaming river,

> Whose islands on its bosom float
> Like emeralds chased in gold.

The same strong touch marks the famous description of a Scottish winter landscape that opens the epistle to William Stewart Rose.

Hitherto I have dwelt rather on the strength of Scott's description, his power of influencing us by impressive natural features, but he was equally susceptible to the softer aspects of nature, and his poems contain descriptive passages of great tenderness and beauty. Instead, however, of adding to the number of set descriptions, I choose as an illustration of

Scott's gentler touch these lines from *County Guy* :

> Ah! County Guy, the hour is nigh,
>   The sun has left the lea,
> The orange-flower perfumes the bower,
>   The breeze is on the sea.
> The lark, his lay who trill'd all day,
>   Sits hush'd his partner nigh;
> Breeze, bird, and flower confess the hour,
>   But where is County Guy?

If now we leave description and turn to narrative, we find the same simplicity of treatment. Scott's art leads him instinctively to select the broad, impressive points, and to set these vividly before the reader. A writer's power in this direction is apt to be severely tried by battle pieces, but this is a test that Scott stands with ease. The battle of Flodden is a masterpiece of simple, clear narrative. The movements of the two armies and the incidents of that fatal day are quickly and easily realised by the reader.

In preceding remarks I have dwelt on the strength of some of Scott's descriptions, and now I would extend that observation to the whole of Scott's work as a poet. He is pre-eminently a strong and stimulating writer. The swift movement of his verse, the bright strong colour of his writing, its romantic glow, its wealth of exciting incident, its finely wrought battle scenes—here is material in abundance for impressive and attractive poetry. As one of Scott's strongest efforts, I would select the charge of the Scots army down Flodden Hill.

> And sudden as he spoke,
> From the sharp ridges of the hill,
> All downward to the banks of Till,
> Was wreathed in sable smoke.
> Volumed and fast, and rolling far,
> The cloud enveloped Scotland's war,
> As down the hill they broke;
> Nor martial shout nor minstrel tone,
> Announced their march; their tread alone,
> At times one warning trumpet blown,
> At times a stifled hum,
> Told England, from his mountain throne
> King James did rushing come.

In another but still a strong vein is the description of Bertram's climb. The reader actually holds his breath as the bold villain scales the beetling cliff.

> Just as the dangerous stretch he makes,
> By heaven, his faithless footstool shakes!
> Beneath his tottering bulk it bends,
> It sways—it loosens—it descends!
> And downward holds its headlong way
> Crashing o'er rock and copsewood spray.

Such passages abound in Scott, who possesses in a pre-eminent degree the power of imparting thrilling excitement.

With this command of the powerful emotions he unites the power of evoking gentler feelings. Naturally the onward sweep of Scott's lines is more in harmony with activity than with the restful feeling of pathos, but time and again his Muse speaks in soft, mournful tones, which sadden while they please. At such times the flow of the verse is checked and the lines move to a gentler music. From the more important poems we might cull many beautiful passages dealing with the chance and change of nature and of life, but the *Violet* is perhaps less well known, and is a beautiful illustration of Scott's softer vein:

> The violet in her greenwood bower,
>   Where birchen boughs with hazels mingle,
> May boast itself the fairest flower
>   In glen, or copse, or forest dingle.
> Though fair her gems of azure hue,
>   Beneath the dew-drop's weight reclining,
> I've seen an eye of lovelier blue
>   More sweet through watery lustre shining.
> The summer sun that dew shall dry
>   Ere yet the day be past its morrow;
> Nor longer in my false love's eye
>   Remained the tear of parting sorrow.

One might dwell on Scott's light and shade as displayed in a whole work, on his delineation of character, on his effective use of nature as a background contrasting or in harmony with the action of the poetry, but enough has been said to show that tried by whatever standard we choose, by his power to appeal to the hearts of his own people, and to win a place in popular admiration, by his claim to rank as a leader in the romantic school, by his intrinsic poetic worth, Scott is and will remain a great poet. As long as the love of nature endures, as long as man delights in old-time memories, as long as our feelings remain fresh and responsive, thus long will Scott's poetry live. It has been charged with faults of omission and commission, but if we look away from these to its positive merits, to its vigour, its glow, its colouring, its picturesque description, and clear, forcible narrative, its light and shade, and its breadth of portraiture, we shall realise how great a poet Scotland gave to the world in Sir Walter Scott.

Zola's Theory of the Novel

ZOLA'S THEORY OF THE NOVEL

To the civilised world Zola was known as the champion of the deeply-injured, much-enduring Dreyfus, to a large part of it as the author of highly realistic novels, to a small number of its inhabitants as a vigorous polemic on the canons of the novel. Like Wordsworth he was not contented merely to apply his method; he must needs expound its principles and maintain them as the best of all possible principles. Both perhaps should have followed the advice given to a novice on the bench by a veteran magistrate, never to give reasons for his decisions.

Zola certainly should. His work as a novelist seems to proceed on lines altogether wrong, but his writing has so much force, so much earnestness, so much concentration of purpose that one easily understands how so many people have been led to rate it as highly as the author did. On the other hand, his exposition of his theory of the novel is full enough and clear enough to convince any one that his palace of art is built on foundations of running sand fatal to any superstructure in proportion to its solidity.

In his critical writings, Zola is a fervent advocate of realism as against idealism, and one may ask, What is realism? A certain Thomas Gradgrind had views on this subject. 'Now,' he said on one occasion, 'what I want is Facts. Teach boys and girls nothing but Facts. Plant nothing else and root out everything else. You can only form the minds of reasoning animals on Facts; nothing else will ever be of any service to them. In this life we want nothing but Facts. We are in all things to be regulated and governed by Fact. We must discard the word Fancy altogether. We have nothing to do with it.' Readers of *Hard Times* know how completely Gradgrind's matter-of-fact policy failed, what misery it brought to himself and to those dependent on him. It may be suggested with relevance and force that the failure of the system in *Hard Times* proves nothing, because the whole combination of circumstances set forth by the novelist is imaginary, but, as will be seen presently, this objection is not open to Zola.

Gradgrind's realism includes an adherence to facts, and a repudiation of fancy. Zola announces in set terms: 'I am simply an observer who ascertains facts.' Again, he says, 'The greatness of a novelist lies in depicting his age not in inventing stories. The great thing is to exhibit living persons playing the comedy of life with the utmost realism.' In order that this may be done, the novelist must collect his facts with the most scrupulous care, and if Zola is asked what facts are to be collected, his reply is that what human nature is capable of is fitting for a novel, and he proceeds to describe what may be found in the newspapers of the day—his summary of news being confined, one observes, to what is brutal, repulsive, or obscene, and the facts are to be treated in a matter-of-fact way. There is no room for the ideal. The whole tendency of the age is declared to be against it; science has declared war against it, and its empire has fallen. Formerly the highest praise one could bestow on a novelist was to say, 'He has imagination.' To-day such language would be regarded almost as censure. All the conditions of novel writing have changed. Imagination is so far now from being the chief quality of the novelist that people have come to see that the ideal is the enemy of the race, encouraging dangerous dreams, alluring to vice, debauching the whole moral system. The ideal does this. To those foolish enough to maintain that it is the realistic writers who fill the mind with coarse and sensual ideas, Zola says, 'You speak stupidly, and without regard to facts. We realistic writers terrify, and do not corrupt. The corrupters are the idealists, who deal in falsehood.' In justice it must be admitted that Zola's realistic novels are not immoral in aim, that they have indeed a most laudable purpose, but the flower safety may be plucked out of less dangerous nettles.

Zola is not so harsh to fancy as Gradgrind, who would discard it altogether. He regards poets as the great representatives of the ideal, but he is magnanimous enough to say that he does not press his triumphant argument in favour of realism so far as to predict the approaching extinction of poetry. 'I assign to poetry,' he says, 'the rôle of an orchestra. The poets may continue to provide music for us while we work.' Which is really a very generous concession!

If we grant for a moment that the province of the novel is the real to the exclusion of the ideal, we may at least comfort ourselves with the reflection that the real includes what is beautiful as well as what is ugly, what is pure as well as what is impure, and that, if novelists are to be confined to the literal truth, they can at least choose what has artistic attractions. In the famous preface to the *Lyrical Ballads*, Wordsworth advocated the right of the poet to use incidents and situations from common life, and to relate or describe them throughout as far as possible in language really employed by men, but his realism produced very different results from Zola's. In such lines as—

> The sun above the mountain's head
>   A freshening lustre mellow
> Through all the long green fields has spread,
>   His first sweet evening yellow,

we get what Zola desiderates—natural facts plainly stated, but we also get what Zola's realism is a stranger to, artistic beauty.

Wordsworth's claim to say whatever is true does not prevent him from dwelling by preference on natural and moral beauty, and it will not do for anyone to say his avoidance of what Zola calls the real was a matter of temperament. It was a matter of method. Wordsworth himself said on one occasion that had he written of love, he would have written with more warmth than his principles would have approved.

Besides agreeing in the demand for reality Wordsworth and Zola are at one in writing with a purpose, but the latter has to reveal what his purpose is; without his explanation not one reader in a thousand is aware of the sternness of his morality. Wordsworth, on the other hand, needs no interpreter. His verse is at times flat and dull whatever be its purpose, but at its best it purifies and elevates, it comforts and sustains by its natural beauty and moral grandeur.

> Time may restore us in its course
> Goethe's sage mind and Byron's force,
> But where will Europe's latter hour
> Again find Wordsworth's healing power?

Wordsworth, however, had heretical ideas about the value of imagination and the poet's duty to give immediate pleasure. Such ideas Zola scorned; they are not for the novelist though they may do for a poet who has no concern with the business of life. His part, it will be remembered, is to provide music while the novelist works.

Yet there are some who, while regarding Zola's realistic subjects with repulsion, and declining to take his purpose seriously, find artistic pleasure in his work. And what yields this pleasure? Why the very qualities Zola shrieks against—his imagination, his command of the ideal world. For this is the Nemesis of the realistic novelist. He forsakes beauty and purity, scornfully leaving them to idealists, and takes by preference what is sordid or foul or ugly. But no sooner has he got his facts than he ceases to be a realist and becomes an idealist. He picks and chooses among his material, rejecting what he dare not use or cannot use effectively, and combining in a purely ideal fashion what he finally selects, the result being an imaginary story, with imaginary characters, imaginary incidents, and imaginary dialogue. And this product of a powerful imagination fed by human documents is what Zola flaunts before the people he calls idealists as an actual transcript of human life. It will not do for Zola to say that his story is a possible one: the point is that it is an imaginary one. As we shall see, Zola admits this, and meets it in a very amusing fashion.

But is Zola's typical realistic novel realistic even in the sense of being possible? Is any average group of human beings so utterly vicious? Are the individuals of the group so like each other in their viciousness? Is their life so limited in interest and so lacking in variety? Both common-sense and experience say 'No.' Not only is Zola's boasted transcript of human life the work of his own imagination; it is the work of an imagination that, while powerful enough, spends its strength within too narrow an area and represents so little of human nature that it caricatures it. Think by way of contrast of Fielding's work. Fielding was a realistic writer who claimed and exercised the right to represent the whole of human life, but then it is the whole of human life he represents. Recall his variety of character, his wealth of incident, his breadth of treatment, the richness of the humour, and the manliness of the style, and then turn to Zola! We see at once how far the latter's novels are from being records of the actual life of actual men and women.

But we have not learned what Zola regards as the supreme function and distinction of the novel. According to him novel-writing, so far from having anything to do with fine art, is one of the applied arts; it is to be classed not with poetry, music, and painting, but with experimental medicine. If, he says, the experimental method leads to knowledge of the physical life, it must also lead to knowledge of the emotional and intellectual life. Here, therefore, is the proper work of the novelist. We have experimental chemistry and physics, then we have experimental physiology, later still we have the experimental novel. It is the business of the experimental novelist to operate on the character and the passions, on the human and social facts as the chemist and the physicist operate on dead matter, as the physiologist operates on living organisms. He must master the mechanism of mental phenomena so as to reveal the machinery behind intellectual and sensual manifestions as determined by heredity and environment, and then he must exhibit men living in the social atmosphere they have themselves produced, which they are always modifying, and by which they are continually being modified. And in carrying on this work the first thing the novelist has to do is to collect his facts; his next step is to select, combine, and modify so as to show the inevitable appearance of a certain result under certain conditions. And here comes in Zola's triumphant reply to those critics who accuse him of departing from absolute truth in his representations of human life. 'Experiment,' he answers, 'involves modification;' which nobody can deny.

And now as to the value of this experimental work. The experimental novelist enquires into the causes of social evil, he analyses individual and social characteristics, he observes, generalises, and records, and finally hands over his collection of human documents to parliament, whose business it becomes to utilise this material for the public benefit by making it the basis of legislation that shall foster what is good and extirpate what is evil. Small wonder that conscious of his mission as a great social reformer, Zola treats with scorn the attacks of critics that persist in regarding him as an artist given to using objectionable materials.

But has this so-called experimental work any such value as Zola assigns to it? Not at all. The whole thing is a dream, as fantastic as anything conceived by the most moon-struck idealist. The whole argument is so completely and absolutely worthless that one hesitates to believe the writer can be in earnest. But to suppose anything else would be to insult Zola, who is nothing if not oppressively serious.

What happens in a real experiment? The experimenter brings about an actual combination of circumstances and produces an actual result, which is independent of him except in so far as he is responsible for the combination. The experimenter, for example, puts into a soda water bottle two volumes of hydrogen and one volume of oxygen and applies a light; water is formed and no gas is left over. Here is an experimental proof of the composition of water. Now compare this with what Zola is pleased to call an experiment. He constructs a story, that is, he brings about a certain combination of circumstances, but it has no real existence like the combination of the hydrogen and the oxygen; it is purely fictitious. In the course of the story we see that certain conduct, that is, a certain combination of circumstances, leads to certain results, but again, the results are fictitious, the creation of the writer. And yet Zola actually compares the fictitious offspring of fictitious circumstances, the figments of his own brain, to the precise and tangible results of sober, scientific work: and upon this flimsy substructure he would have parliaments rear a new social order. One might as well try to build a lighthouse on the sea foam, or to cross Niagara on moonbeams.

And while refusing to accept Zola's realistic novels as valuable contributions to sociology, one may be sceptical of their tendency to terrify from vice. For the same objection holds good here also; the whole belongs to the realm of fiction and the value of any moral lesson that may be suggested is thereby very much discounted. Speaking of *The Old Curiosity Shop*, Mr. Forster says, 'many an over-suspicious person will find advantage in remembering what a too liberal application of Foxey's principle of suspecting everybody brought Mr. Sampson Brass to; and many an over-hasty judgment of poor human nature will unconsciously be checked, when it is remembered that Mr. Christopher Nubbles *did* come back to work out that shilling.' This is more than doubtful. The argument that a didactic purpose is fatal to the novel as a work of art would not have struck Zola as relevant, but one may urge the superiority of biography or history to fiction as a fount of moral instruction; their examples have the advantage of being *real*.

A good deal of Zola's reasoning involves the assumption that realism is a thing of to-day, the child of modern science, which has given the ideal its death-blow. As a matter of fact, realism was a potent influence in literature long before the day of modern experimental science; instead of being a permanent and dominating tendency established in these last days, realism is simply an aspect of art that receives in alternation with other aspects special attention at special epochs. Had Zola never read *La Réalisme et Le Naturalisme*, by his countryman, A. David-Sauvageot? In that masterly sketch of the history of realism he would have found abundant evidence that realism, instead of delaying its advent till the birth of modern science, is as old as literature itself. The ebb and flow of the tendency is well marked in the records of the English novel. Aphra Behn's *Oroonoko* appeared in 1668 and marked the rising of a tide of realism that made its influence felt far into the eighteenth century. Now the Royal Society had been founded six years earlier, but it is more instructive to observe that this epoch of realistic novel writing succeeded an epoch in which the romantic novel had become so swollen with bombastic extravagance that it actually lost the power of motion, and the realistic epoch was succeeded in its turn by the wildly romantic stories of the School of Terror, the *Castle of Otranto*, the *Mysteries of Udolpho*, the *Old English Baron*, etc.

The fact is, there are times or moods in the history of nations, as of individuals, when the loftier ideals are unpalatable, when Spenser is laid aside in favour of Crabbe, when a keener relish is found in realism, which is only the ideal working at a lower level. Sound taste simply asks that each form shall be genuine; that the novel, for example, shall not be a menstruum for a sermon or a polemic. Thus Thackeray is taken and Zola left; because the former is the truer artist, and *therefore* is the better teacher. If at times he seems too fond of tracing pleasing human actions to a root of selfishness, too fond of stirring the soil in order to show us the corruption beneath from which some fair flower has sprung, he is always in sympathy with the best of human nature and glad to think mankind is capable of disinterested actions and emotions altogether pure. His broader treatment is due to a delicate sense of proportion and a strong sense of humour. Of this latter sense, as has been suggested, Zola has none, and hence his novels contain passages that are amusing rather than striking.

While Thackeray confined himself within moderate limits, trying to reproduce human life as he saw it, shrinking with acute sensitiveness from exaggerating the good and the evil in man, he would have smiled at Zola's idea of the novelist as a scientific experimenter feeding parliaments with human documents. His is a less ambitious but a more useful function. While we admire his artistic skill, we have searchings of heart as we follow his delineation of the workings of the human soul; for one that is terrified by Zola's gloomy and repulsive pictures, thousands are reproved by Thackeray's satirical exposure of the errors and frailties of the race. And he achieves this result without sacrificing art in the vain pursuit of purpose, and without disfiguring his pages by minute description of scenes condemned by every law of art or taste or ethics.

BIBLIOLIFE

Old Books Deserve a New Life
www.bibliolife.com

Did you know that you can get most of our titles in our trademark **EasyScript**™ print format? **EasyScript**™ provides readers with a larger than average typeface, for a reading experience that's easier on the eyes.

Did you know that we have an ever-growing collection of books in many languages?

Order online:
www.bibliolife.com/store

Or to exclusively browse our **EasyScript**™ collection:
www.bibliogrande.com

At BiblioLife, we aim to make knowledge more accessible by making thousands of titles available to you – quickly and affordably.

Contact us:
BiblioLife
PO Box 21206
Charleston, SC 29413

Lightning Source UK Ltd.
Milton Keynes UK
05 August 2010

157712UK00001BC/2/A